The Hazards of Theology:
Reaping the Benefits,
Avoiding the Pitfalls

THE HAZARDS OF THEOLOGY

Reaping the Benefits, Avoiding the Pitfalls

By Geoffrey F. Spencer

Herald Publishing House
Independence, Missouri

Copyright 1997
Herald Publishing House
Independence, Missouri

Printed in the United States of America

Library of Congress Cataloging-in-Publication Data
Geoffrey F. Spencer
   The hazards of theology : reaping the benefits, avoiding the pit-
falls / by Geoffrey F. Spencer.
   Includes bibliographical references and index.
   ISBN 0-8309-0772-6
   1. Reorganized Church of Jesus Christ of Latter Day Saints—Doc-
trines—Study and teaching.   2. Theology—Methodology. I. Title.
BX8675.S64   1997   97-1612
230'.93—dc21   CIP

01 00 99 98 97   1 2 3 4 5

Table of Contents

Dedicated
to the memory of
Paul Haworth Henricks (1917–1995)
Mentor, Benefactor, and Friend
In profound gratitude for an association
that spanned two continents and half a century

Foreword

The church, first and foremost, is a theological community, seeking truth through the gift of faith and the discipline of study, and endeavoring to implement the truth as perceived in the world which is the fruit of God's creative impulse and the object of God's love.

In this brief study I have attempted, albeit modestly, to describe the nature of the theological enterprise, particularly as understood and practiced in the Reorganized Church of Jesus Christ of Latter Day Saints. Although we have come to sense how deeply we are indebted to the larger Christian community through time, we bring our own particular history and experience to the task, and at our best magnify the legacy bequeathed us by our forebears, who in their time laid down some remarkably wise principles to guide the theological task. To the extent that we have observed those guidelines, the church has been blessed: in the measure that we have been slow to learn, the outcome has been tragic, both for individuals and the institution as a whole.

The exploration of specific theological issues, or study of theological "schools," is outside the scope of this book, except for the sake of illustration. I have primarily attempted to show how history, tradition, precedent, and conference actions inform our present practice of theology. Necessarily, the references will be limited largely to Restoration writers of earlier vintage, though not exclusively. The continuing invitation to theological inquiry must rest in younger and more competent hands.

The book contains these elements:

1. The written text, for private or group study.

2. Discussion questions for each session, primarily for class use.

3. Activities for the reader, provided on the assumption that theology is an active discipline, something one *does*, even more than something one *has*. It is suggested that students plan to keep the results of the several activities under one cover, as far as possible, with the hope that the assignments, if completed, will form a helpful resource in itself.

4. Three previews, more to stimulate interest than as any kind of rigorous test. Anybody can devise tests that would be difficult for others to "pass." The purpose of these previews is rather to suggest the breadth of the field of theology and its related disciplines, and to hint at paths that might be pursued according to the reader's interests.

5. A case study, inviting the reader, or group of readers, to undertake an actual examination of one aspect of Reorganization faith that has been largely neglected. This is intended to provide an opportunity for theological dialogue carried out with intellectual discipline and active faith.

I would like to think that this brief offering will make a small contribution to our competent practice of theology and to a fruitful praxis, which is the proper duty and calling of the church. This is what I should like it to be, for the church has been the source of my blessing and the object of my affection for virtually the entire course of my life.

Geoff Spencer

Note: By the very nature of this study, I have made frequent reference to two sources in particular. The first is *The History of the Reorganized Church of Jesus Christ of Latter Day Saints*, published in eight volumes. I have consistently referred to this source more briefly as *Church History*. The second is the Reorganization's general periodical which has been published under two names, *The True Latter Day Saints' Herald* and the *Saints Herald*. Where it can be done without confusing the reader, I will simply use the abbreviated term *Herald*.

Chapter 1

Inquiring Minds Want to Know

> **I,**
> **Why?**
>
> — Reportedly the second shortest
> poem in the English language

> **All this man-made thinking about what we believe doesn't**
> **help me one bit. In fact, it only confuses me. I prefer just**
> **to read the scriptures and have faith. Then if I need to**
> **know anything God will make it known to me.**
> — Overheard in a church foyer

> **I love flowers, but I hate botany; I love religion, but I**
> **hate theology.**
> — Purported translation of hieroglyphics discovered
> on the wall of an ancient Egyptian burial chamber

Theology: Challenge to Faith?

Theology has not enjoyed a favorable image or reputation in recent years. In religious settings it has often suffered a poor press. There has been a tendency, though not so prevalent as it was some years ago, to dismiss theology as impractical, separated from real life, promoting doubt, or even improper for people of faith. "We sent our son to the church college to strengthen everything that we had tried to pass on to him,"

11

complains a devoted church family, "and he came home with all those strange ideas which were undermining his faith."

These parents reflect the point of view that somehow theology threatens belief and may destroy the foundations on which faith is built. And so it is considered more fruitful to hold to a simple, undoubting faith rather than continually submitting beliefs to probing and questioning. Far better, the argument runs, to hold to the simple gospel that we have always believed without stirring up doubts and divisions by raising all these questions.

The gospel may be "simple" in the sense that no person is prevented from receiving the good news because of lack of education, seniority, experience, or sophistication. The gospel may be experienced in appropriate and significant ways by a one-year-old child—perhaps earlier, if what we are learning about prenatal experience is valid. However, the ability to respond intelligently to all the varied circumstances and choices of life is not simple. From the earliest experience of the primitive church in dealing with the question of gentile converts, Christians have struggled with the meaning of the gospel and its application in specific situations. Moreover, good people of righteous intent have often found it necessary to exercise charity in working out differences. Faith may indeed be simple, uncluttered by pretense and minutia, but it need not be simplistic.

The apostle Paul expressed genuine sorrow for fellow Jews who, in his opinion, "have a zeal for God, but it is not enlightened" (Romans 1:2 RSV). A more recent observer has described some Christians as having a great deal of heat, but not much light. Strong, even impassioned feelings or convictions cannot serve as an adequate substitute for informed and reasoned understanding. Thus, another of the New Testament writers advised the early disciples to "be ready at any time to give a quiet and reverent answer to any man who wants a reason for the hope that you have within you" (I Peter 3:15, Phillips). It is by no means unusual that those who can give a "quiet and reverent answer" to inquirers outside their denominational community will have a great deal of difficulty in doing the same when differences of opinion surface within the faith. In recent years it is such differences, those within faith communities, that have stirred the most heated controversy and illustrated some of the hazards of theological dialogue.

Some are convinced that it is how one *feels*, rather than the ideas that may be developed, that is the most important consideration. Ideas can lead you astray, such people insist, but you can trust your feelings. The notion is that ideas can be distorted by all kinds of prejudices and motivations, while there is a directness and purity about feelings that elevates them above theology. If the feelings are strong, and accompanied by what has sometimes been referred to as "the burning in the bosom" or "being given to know," then all other matters are secondary. Such feelings carry their own built-in authority and render theological scrutiny superfluous and disrespectful. Responding to this criticism of theology, Daniel Migliori has observed:

> Christian faith must not be reduced to a euphoric feeling or a homiletic cliché.... The sort of thinking that Christian faith sets in motion does not replace trust in God but acts as a critical ingredient that helps to distinguish faith from mere illusion or pious evasion.[1]

The relationship of religious experience to theology is a critical consideration, and one that will be explored in more detail in chapter 3.

It is not at all uncommon to encounter the criticism of theology that it is a merely human product that can only debase and distort divine revelation. This is profoundly misleading. On the one hand it fails to recognize that our interpretation and expression of the revelatory experience is itself also a human product. On the other hand it implies that human knowledge, wisdom, and judgment are somehow untrustworthy. A person may say: "I just preach, teach, and believe the plain gospel as it comes straight from God's word in the scriptures, rather than getting caught up in the man-made intricacies of theology. I prefer to accept the truth as it is communicated directly to me." However, this person is also expressing a theological stance, perhaps unaware of the fact, but nevertheless formidable. Arthur Oakman once acknowledged the primary function of revelation, while cautioning against the temptation to equate scripture or doctrinal statements with revelation:

> There are, strictly speaking, no revealed truths. There are "truths of revelation"—statements of principles which stem from the actual revelatory experience. These may be, like the map guides to the beatific vision—but they are not the vision itself.... Sacred writings and formulated statements of doctrine are neither the substance nor the reality of revelation. They are records of the divine acts in which the revelation was given, or they are the formulated statement of faith.... Statements of belief (such as are found, for instance, in Doctrine and Covenants 17) are not themselves revelation, but compilations of inferences drawn from the living experience with God....[2]

Again, the relationship between the perception of revelatory experience and the statements that issue forth from one's interpretation of that experience is an important consideration, and will be taken up in chapter 4.

In a cultural environment that places high value on action and prizes the "movers and shakers," theology may be discounted as a mere "head trip" for those without the ability or courage to act. Thus, with a slight amendment to a saying (which is itself questionable), critics will claim: "Those who can, do; those who can't, theologize." Certainly, Christian faith calls for faithful response to the demands of the gospel; to lives of service and faithful discipleship. This should be considered intelligent and relevant action, growing out of careful reflection on the foundations in the gospel. Although the gospel may be a call to action, the church repeatedly considers at length and with differences of opinion, what those appropriate actions are. It is important to *do*, but knowing what to do is more than a matter of instinct or reflex action. Knowing *what* to do is much more likely to follow some careful reflection, or *theologizing*. For instance, one might readily accept the injunction to love the neighbor, but it might not be immediately and automatically obvious with what actions the love is to be expressed. Even the lawyer's question: "Who is my neighbor?" was a theological question, which Jesus saw fit to answer.

Indeed, there are times when it might be appropriate, even preferable, to set the old adage on its ear. Instead of exhorting, "Don't just stand there, do something," it might be more productive to say, "Don't just do something, stand there." If the standing permits thought to determine the best and most effective action, then the advice would be sound. Again, to quote Migliori:

> Questionable indeed is the theology whose theory is no longer linked to transforming praxis. But the criticism is one-sided. If theory without praxis is empty, praxis without theory is blind. How are Christians to know whether this or that action is "for the sake of Christ and the coming kingdom of God" if they impatiently shrug off the questions: Who is Christ? and What is his kingdom? Mindless leaps into action are no more Christian than thinking for thinking's sake.... There is a creative waiting as well as a creative acting.[3]

1. How would you respond to the person (cited at the beginning of this chapter) who is critical of "man-made thinking" about God? What kind of doctrine of revelation is implied in this statement?

2. Discuss Arthur Oakman's distinction between "revealed truths" and "truths of revelation." What caution is he attempting to raise? What is the practical significance of this distinction for theological discussion?

3. What is the meaning of the term "inference" in the statement by Oakman? Give examples of inferences from everyday life. What is its significance when applied to theology?

What's in a Word?

Mention of the term *praxis* (customary practice or conduct) in the preceding quotation draws attention to another objection to theology, especially to theological language. It is not uncommon to hear the observation that "some people like to show off their superiority by using fancy jargon." Now clearly the use of technical or unfamiliar terms for the sake of elevating one's own importance is foolish and aggravating. But the fact is that theology, like every other branch of knowledge, does have a range of terms specific to its discipline. Those who wish to communicate in the fields of medicine, automotive engineering, plumbing, or any other discipline will spend hundreds of hours becoming proficient in the language. Similarly, those who are interested in football, fishing, antiques, or guns will gladly learn the "language" in order to understand what they read and to be able to communicate with others interested in that field. In the contemporary world, young children learn early that computer language is the doorway to competence. It would appear that the willingness and ability to learn a particular language, whether it be Spanish or aeronautical engineering (or theology), is directly related to the measure of interest and commitment invested in the subject. I have known people who objected to the language of theology, but would nevertheless spend significant time and effort to become proficient in the language of astronomy, or combustion engines, or fly fishing with the greatest of sophistication.

When I inquired of my daughter what was meant by the term "beta blocker" and why people couldn't use a simpler word, I was informed that those in the field of medicine understand it, and that it would take many more words to explain it. "That's just what it's called," she said, "and everybody who needs to know understands it." Similarly, while a stranger to the game of cricket might wish for plainer terms than "silly mid-on" or "short fine leg" those terms are immediately intelligible to those who have learned the discipline. It would be difficult to explain them without using a great many more words. Making a slight adaptation of the biblical statement, it might properly be said that "where your heart is, there will your vocabulary be also."

The field of religion is no different, and in many instances is more demanding. For not only will many terms have specialized meaning (such as "justification") but the same terms will often be used with varying shades of meaning. Unless great care is taken with the language, people might easily talk past each other in a conversation or argument. As G. K. Chesterton once remarked, observing two housewives arguing over their neighboring back fence: "Those two will never understand each other because they are arguing from different premises." Even apparently simple terms such as love, salvation, spiritual, or revelation may be readily accepted and used because they have become commonplace and yet may be used without much thought to their meaning(s), or to the varied nuances that might be attached to them.

At the risk of laboring the point, the term "praxis" might serve as a good example in the field of theology. The term implies more than practice; it connotes action or behavior that is consistent with some standard of conduct or principle. It has a specific meaning for which it is difficult to find substitutes, and can communicate immediately and accurately.

4. Where is your heart (interest, passionate concern)? How adequately do you possess the language that goes with your interest or interests? In the field of theology do you have the vocabulary that enhances communication? How did you come by that language, and are you still developing your language?

5. Can you give examples of theological terms that might sometimes be used by other RLDS members with different meanings? By members of other Christian faiths? How can communication be improved under these circumstances?

Faith Seeking Understanding

Perhaps at this point it is timely to consider the meaning of the word "theology." Howard Booth, a Graceland College professor, writes:

> Few of us function as professional theologians, but all of us who identify with and participate in the Christian community are called to disciplined thinking about the nature of our religious or theological affirmations. Reflection on our faith convictions and experience is theology. We can't escape theologizing.... Theological systems are ways of explaining the significance and meaning of life's experiences.[4]

In the first place, it will be helpful to acknowledge that theology is something one *does*, rather than something one *has*, like an object or possession. In this respect it is probably more accurate to speak of *theologizing*, as does Howard Booth, to underscore the active nature of the discipline. Here at least there is an active term, whereas when we need to emphasize faith as an active process, there is no English equivalent, unless we invent the word *faithing*.

A second preliminary comment may not be out of place. Theologizing is something we will be doing whether we admit it or not, and whether we are conscious of it or not. Indeed, a person in the very act of denying theology may, in fact, be theologizing, because he or she may be expressing a view about how one should express one's beliefs. As soon as an individual became aware of being an "I," the question arose, "I! Why?" The questions relating to identity, meaning, origins, and purpose are religious questions which at some level, no matter how rudimentary, such an individual will ask. Theology, then, may be understood as the response that Christians make (as well as others, in their own framework of meaning) to work out the meaning of their lives in terms of values, principles, commitments, and responses. The Christian will ask, consciously or not: What does God's saving action mean in terms of the way I understand and live in the world?" At best it is the ongoing effort to make coherent sense of ourselves, others, and our world.

Theology is an activity that does not stand in opposition to faith, or faithing, but arises from and is prompted by the relationship of faith. It is, as Anselm stated, "faith seeking understanding," the disciplined effort to think through and articulate the implications of one's faith. The relationship between faith, belief, and statements of doctrine requires further examination, which will be taken up in chapter 4.

---

5. Discuss Howard Booth's description of theology as "disciplined thinking." What kinds of discipline are involved in this process? In your life? What kind of "life experiences" do you reflect on in working out your theological understandings?
6. Is it possible to have some kind of faith *without* understanding? What would it look like? What other sources do you call on in seeking a coherent framework and sense of purpose for your life?

There is, it needs to be said, a critical or questioning dimension to theology. In the first place, theology is necessarily a questioning process because we are confronting foundational issues, and the answers are not self-evident. If we are honest and take time to think about it, life is a mystery in terms of its origins, meaning, and destiny. Of course, the assumption that there *is* a meaning and a destiny is itself a theological statement.

Further, the meanings that I may develop must be meanings *for me*. I cannot assign a delegate to do my thinking and reach my conclusions, though I may seek the help of others. My theology cannot consist of a series of unexamined assertions handed down from some authority, to which I assent in such a way that I am saved the discipline and energy of thought. Spiritual "fast food" may be secured with a minimum of effort and may serve to assuage an immediate need, but it will not be an adequate diet to stand up under the demands of living life intelligently, faithfully, and fruitfully. Such a commitment necessarily involves questioning, rather than rote learning and memorizing answers. Touching on this theme, Arthur Oakman made the following bold statement many years ago: "Anyway, people grow in intellectual stature and spiritual power in direct proportion to the quality of the queries they raise, not the answers they are able to give."[5]

One small detail in a well-known story, included as an insert in the Inspired Version, illustrates the significance of the questioning attitude. In identifying the three disciples who accompanied Jesus on the Mount of Transfiguration (Mark 9:2 IV, 9:1 others) the text inserts the words: "who asked him many questions concerning his sayings." Whatever the origin of the addition, the inference quite reasonably to be drawn from this statement is that the searching mind is rewarded with the most revealing experiences.

So the theological process is interrogative by nature; it presumes a readiness on the part of its practitioners to question and to be questioned. While the theologian—each one of us— will stand at any point on strongly held convictions, he or she will be aware that questions tend to open up the continuing search, while answers may close it off.

7. Evaluate Arthur Oakman's statement about questions and answers. Do you think the position is over-stated? Do the educational experiences among adults in your congregation give proper value to questions, or is the main concern to establish answers?
8. What are the sources that have brought you to your present stage in the theological journey? Can you identify written materials, individuals, or situations that have had a significant impact along the way?

Ten Considerations for the Theologian

Abiding by the conviction that every person who gives even rudimentary consideration to the questions of existence is acting as a theologian, I list here several basic guidelines for the process. Some, though not necessarily all, will be taken up and discussed in more detail at subsequent points throughout this book.

1. Each person needs to be engaged in the theological task as a personal stewardship and responsibility. It cannot be delegated to representatives, to the presiding officers, to a committee, or to professional theologians.

2. No person can effectively theologize alone. It is a personal task, but never exclusively a private one. Each person's viewpoint and resources will be important, but no single person's contribution will be sufficient. The principle of synergy suggests that all of us together are likely to think more effectively than any one of us alone.

3. It is not possible to engage in the theological process exclusively by telling or by listening. There might be times or occasions when one mode predominates, but the best growth takes place when people participate in both modes. Both attitudes must be adopted seriously and not merely for the sake of appearance.

4. In connection with the preceding, the process must be characterized by mutual respect and tolerance: people must be free to participate openly, freely, and without fear of "put downs."

5. Theology is more than a set of ideas or statements of belief. It is even more importantly a method for dealing with crucial situations and choices. It is in the interplay between beliefs and life situations that the truth takes shape. The theological task must never wander too far afield from the active life and concerns of individuals and communities. In the midst of any theological discussion it will always be helpful to have somebody ask: "What does this mean for us, *here* and *now*, both in this congregation and in the world around us?"

6. Theology must be acquainted with and take into account the tradition. The basic questions have been struggled with for two millennia, and some sound insights have actually emerged over that period, although members of the church have often considered that large blocks of history had nothing worthwhile to offer. Of course, the tradition embraces that part of the story that is particularly ours as members of the Restoration movement and of the Reorganization. At the same time, that part of the tradition should be subjected to question and challenge, no matter how hallowed by time or authority.

7. Theology must be aware of the temptation to ideology. When the temptation to maintain the system becomes a way of preserving the power and status or comfort of those who benefit from it, the theological process has been subverted.

8. There will be a balance, even a tension, between conviction and modesty or tentativeness. Each person will act on the best that he or she knows, while recognizing that no formulation of the faith is ultimate, final, and perfect.

9. The theological process involves learning by study *and also* by faith, not as alternative paths to understanding but as necessary companions (Doctrine and Covenants 85:36a).

10. Effective theological "work" follows from sound schol-

22

arship, if not in the strict academic sense at least in terms of careful and deliberate habits of thought and study. Whether as a personal activity, or in the dialogue of the community, this will mean more than the casual, ad hoc take-it-or-leave-it process that bedevils too many of our church school classes and other educational settings. In a culture that emphasizes entertainment and a casual approach to any disciplined endeavor, the educational process has suffered, both with adults and children.

The opinion, stated at the outset, that religion is something to be admired and valued, whereas theology is something to be despised or ignored, is quite common, and in many specific instances may be justified. Theology (or rather the bad practice of it) may be pompous, obscure, dull, and even acrimonious, provoking disruptions in human relationships and achieving little in the process. However, as William Hordern has pointed out: "The answer to poor theology must be good theology, not no theology. We can see why this is if we analyze what theology is."[6]

Activities for the Reader

A. Decide on one important matter about which you are currently asking some searching questions, with the possible outcome of revising your understanding. State this concern in writing as clearly as possible. Then state, also as clearly as you can
  - why you are reconsidering the matter;
  - what resources or procedures, if any, you are using in your reevaluation; and
  - why the matter is important to you.
B. Read an article of some substance from the *Saints Herald*, a book, or a journal on religion. If none of the above is available, choose what appears to be a report or statement from your local newspaper. Then do the following:

- Write a brief statement summarizing the thesis or purpose of the selection.
- Add a brie statement indicating whether or not you agree with the position stated and why.
- State what you consider to be the theological implications of the selection.
- Choose another person with whom to discuss the selection. State your thoughts on the matter to your partner. Then listen carefully while your partner expresses a viewpoint. Share what you learn from the conversation with your partner.

Notes

1. Daniel Migliori, *Faith Seeking Understanding* (Grand Rapids, Michigan: William B. Eerdmans, 1991), 7.
2. Arthur Oakman, "Theology, Its Place and Meaning," *Saints' Herald* 113, no. 9 (May 1, 1966): 313.
3. Migliori, 8.
4. Howard Booth, "The Task of Theology," *Saints Herald* 136, no. 7 (July 1989): 279.
5. Arthur Oakman, *The Central Witness of the Book of Mormon*, The Gospel Quarterly, vol. 17, no. 1 (Independence, Missouri: Herald House, 1948), author's preface.
6. William Hordern, *A Layman's Guide to Protestant Theology* (New York: MacMillan, 1959), 1.

Chapter 2

Why Hazardous?

"Some of you have sought security in the words and phrases by which the faithful of earlier days have expressed their knowledge of me."
—Doctrine and Covenants 149:4

"Wouldn't you know it. Just when it looks like we have got over all the upset caused by one strange idea, somebody comes up with another one. Where is it all going to end?"
—Brother A to Sister B

The title of this book, and of this chapter, makes an assertion that might not be immediately self-evident—that there are pitfalls and difficulties attached to the theological process. How can it be that an activity so basic to discipleship and the search for truth often resembles a minefield, with hazards for even the most well-intentioned practitioner? Golfers are well aware that the term hazard is applied to certain aspects of the golf course, not the least of which are the sand traps that invariably surround each hole or the areas designated out of bounds. Such hazards, not to mention the bodies of water that seem to act like magnets to golf balls, may frustrate the best-intentioned golfer. The hazards in theology are no less real, and generally far more disastrous in their effects. In this chapter I will attempt to identify and explore some of the factors that have created friction and divisions over the centuries between Christians of different faiths and among those of the same faith.

The American Heritage Dictionary of the English Language provides several meanings for the word "hazard," at least two of which have a direct bearing on the practice of theology. In the first place, a hazard is defined as a danger, peril, or risk. Hopefully some of the perils of the theological process will become evident in the course of this chapter. But the term also may be applied to a chance event or an accident. Hazards in theology often arise from the unconscious or accidental failure to maintain sound principles, which govern the process. Yet, the results of hazards can be extremely unfortunate.

These hazards are not to be minimized and certainly not ignored. They strike not only at the ideas we profess, but at the relationships that exist between people. They have caused rifts within families, splintered denominations, frequently spilled over into the political arena, and often erupted in conflict and bloodshed. Although most people who read this book will probably only encounter the hazards in their more benign form, they are nevertheless formidable and call all of us as practicing theologians to protect and preserve the process at its highest level.

Sensitive Issues and Sensitive People

Theological issues, if they are worthy of our consideration, tend to cut right to the heart of our treasured convictions. They deal with more than matters of casual opinion, or taste. They are generally more than mere interesting topics of conversation. Such convictions we experience as an expression of our own personhood. It demands discipline on our part not to interpret attacks on our treasured ideas as personal assaults, as a diminution of who we are, and a threat to our security or status. The highways of theology are strewn with the bodies of those who were just "defending the truth."

We are deeply invested in our own ideas. Whether or not we have come to those ideas by great efforts of time and study, we may nevertheless feel offended if they do not appear to engender the same loyalty we have exhibited. One theologian has sometimes referred to the process as "bleeding in public," a vivid way of pointing to the sensitivity and even pain we may feel when risking our ideas in the marketplace.

As a member of the committee producing *Hymns of the Saints* (Herald House, 1981), I recall how difficult it was to inform individuals that their offering of a hymn text was not accepted for inclusion. It was as if a part of the individual had been violated. As one who submitted several texts for the committee's consideration, I confess to feeling the same anxiety, and appreciating the fact that if a text was not accepted, the name of the author remained unknown, as a protection against possible hurt. Had my name been made public before or during consideration of a text, both the committee and I would have felt we were under some constraint. Members of the committee might have hesitated to express their true opinion in my presence, and I would have felt vulnerable to criticism.

As respectful as we might endeavor to be, such protections are not at our disposal in theological discussion, nor can they be. Ideas and opinions are openly shared, and our sensitive feelings are at the mercy of the community. People who express their opinions through letters, as to the *Saints Herald*, may not feel the sting of face-to-face discussion, but still render themselves vulnerable to the strong opinions of others, as the Letters column amply illustrates.

Given these factors, theological discussion should be carried out with a mutual sensitivity. People must be free to speak candidly, without fear of ridicule, condemnation, or hostility. Theological dialogue, unless it is content to be as Roy Cheville once pointed out, "a bland shuffling of our prejudices," is dialogue at a very high level of maturity.

1. Can you recall any occasion when an idea of yours was ridiculed, rejected, or judged as false? How did you feel (a) within yourself? (b) toward your antagonists? Do you feel you are able to engage in serious theological discussions without feelings of threat or hostility?
2. Sometimes people will advance the opinion that it is better just to ignore potentially divisive issues rather than risk the discomfort of strained relationships. Discuss the positive and negative elements in adopting this stance in theological discussion in your congregation.

In My Humble Opinion

Whether theological views have been developed with considerable discipline and effort, or have arrived by "happenstance," people are most likely to give a great deal of credence to their own convictions. It is difficult for anyone to say "I may be wrong" and really mean it. In fact, the statement often carries with it a heavy overtone of skepticism, as if the very idea that we could be in error is just too absurd to be taken seriously. Apart from the suspected loss of prestige or the damage to our self-image, a genuine admission of the possibility of error carries with it the obligation to change one's mind, or to go back to the drawing board to think further.

A former president of the Council of Twelve, for whom I have had a great deal of respect, would remind his colleagues from time to time that virtually every statement, certainly about religious matters, may be described as a "truth-lie." Any such statement purporting to explain ultimate truth would by its nature contain at the same time elements of truth and untruth, or "less-than-truth." No statement, be it about God, the Holy

Spirit, creation, love, salvation, atonement, resurrection, eternal life, or any other, can be perfectly immaculate, without the possibility of any element of "other-than-truth" or "less-than-truth."

What this means is that every person's ideas and statements will be a mixture, unless that person claims the ability to speak with the tongues of angels, or more. If so, modesty is not out of place—in fact, the theologian will proceed with the basic assumption that even her or his best ideas are touched with mortality, both by the limitations of language and the imperfections of human beings. There is no such thing, theologically, as an "immaculate concept." Although the report of a language that was "pure and undefiled" (Genesis 6:6 IV) gained some note in the early years of the Restoration, it is difficult to perceive what that language might have been, and it is certain that no contemporary has mastered it.

The Power of Feelings

Because theology, at its best, deals with basic issues rather than peripheral or inconsequential ones, and people tend to attach a great deal of authority to their feelings as a guide to truth, those feelings are highly influential in validating or condemning views. "I feel so strongly about it that I just know it must be right," a person might say. On the other hand, another might say of the same idea: "That idea leaves me so cold I just know it can't be right, however convincing your arguments might seem." This means that theological issues can quickly become emotionally laden. The role of feeling or experience will be examined further in the next chapter. Suffice it to say here that the deep investment of personal feelings in theological dialogue may not only constitute a threat to the ability of those individuals to consider issues with some degree of objectivity, but can interfere in the interchange of ideas in good spirit which is basic to productive dialogue.

3. Discuss the notion of a "pure and undefiled" language. Would this mean that all the terms of the vocabulary had absolutely clear and "uncontaminated" meanings? Or does it mean that the people using the language were perfect in concepts and character? Do you think such a language, if it were possible, would make theological discussion easier?

4. Can you recall a situation where matters, especially of a religious nature, were discussed in an atmosphere of highly charged feelings? This may have occurred in an informal group, in some more formal way in the congregation, or at a conference. How did the feelings affect the quality of the discussion? What happened, if anything, to the personal relationships of the people engaged in the debate? Would any other outcome have been possible?

The Christian and Prejudice

Prejudice may be defined as a strong tendency to categorize people on the basis of some arbitrarily selected, and largely irrelevant, characteristic. Prejudicial thinking will be directed toward other races, religions, socioeconomic groups, or toward the opposite gender. It is particularly operative when individuals or groups perceive a threat to the satisfaction of their needs, especially the need for status or security, or the comfort of being right.

The strength of prejudice may reflect (albeit not acknowledged) distrust, fear, or hostility toward the other. Often the prejudice will be exhibited in disguised and outwardly benign forms: "Our next door neighbors are Catholics, but they are very nice people." Unspoken is the assumption that Catholics are generally other than "nice" people, so that the unusual quality of the neighbors calls for a special comment. What would be the reaction to those who might say, "Our neighbors are RLDS, but they really are quite normal people"?

Prejudice may be active in another way. Harvey Cox has written: "All thinking, including theological thinking, arises *in part* as ideology; that is the defense of this or that institution's power and privilege."[1] When the defense of one's beliefs and institution becomes the dominating force or influence behind theological dialogue in the "in-group," it will be difficult to look at one's own affiliation clearly and to represent other "out-groups" accurately. The temptation is to set up "straw-men" as if they were faithful representations of other groups, and then establish one's superiority by contrast. It is difficult indeed to distance oneself from one's own interests and prestige.

Some years ago (1972) Andrew Greeley, himself a cleric, stated that: "The research findings on the connection between religion and prejudice are overwhelming." This was in concert with an earlier study carried out by sociologist Gordon Allport that concluded, on the basis of his research, that "on the average, churchgoers are more intolerant than nonchurchgoers." A later study conducted by Daniel Batson and Larry Ventis (1982) reached the conclusion that, at least for white middle-class Christians in the United States, religion was not associated with increased love and acceptance but with increased intolerance, prejudice, and bigotry. This could suggest either that Christianity appeals to those with a prejudiced disposition or that affiliation with a religious organization cultivates prejudiced feelings. Whatever it might be, the conclusions should be disturbing to church-going individuals.

Perhaps we would all like to take exception to these conclusions, possibly from the conviction of our own personal freedom from intolerance. Many might want to assert that "there's not a prejudiced bone in my body." Nevertheless, the strength of misapplication of the "chosen people" image, the tendency among Christians, at least, toward particularism, and the need for status, security, and the comfort of being right, or more right than anybody else, should serve as warnings that prejudice is a formidable hindrance to the theological quest.

5. The author suggests that a common expression of prejudice is the judgment against other or "out-groups" based on false generalizations or misinformation. Do you think the RLDS Church has sometimes been the victim of such prejudicial conduct? If so, how do you feel when such attacks come to your attention, in the public media or otherwise? Do you think members of the church might at times have been perpetrators of the same kind of acts toward "gentiles," Utah Mormons, others? How can such habits be minimized?

6. To what extent do you consider accurate the criticism by Batson and Ventis toward white middle-class Christians in the U.S.? If valid, is such prejudice increasing or decreasing in our contemporary culture? What evidence supports your opinion?

It is highly questionable that the completely unprejudiced individual exists. However, the mere recognition of our own vulnerability should help to lower the level of prejudice. It is revealing to note that the contention of James Dittes, another researcher, that highly active members of churches are among the least prejudiced, while the marginally active are among the most prejudiced.[2] In effect, the way individuals integrate religious convictions and practices into their lives makes a significant difference. An earlier study by Gordon Allport, in proposing six criteria for a mature religious faith, included the value of a well-differentiated belief system, subject to constant examination, and a stance of problem-solving, searching for growing understanding. If this is indeed true, the significance of an energetic theological dialogue is evident.

The Pain of Change

Perhaps the most formidable hazard encountered in the theological journey is the pain of change. M. Scott Peck, co-recipient with his wife of the 1994 Temple Peace Award, expressed this problem in his now-classic book, *The Road Less Traveled*:

> Our view of reality is like a map with which to negotiate the terrain of life. If the map is true and accurate, we will generally know where we are, and if we have decided where to go, we will generally know how to get there.... While this is obvious, it is something that most people to a greater or lesser degree choose to ignore. They ignore it because our route to reality is not easy. First of all, we are not born with maps; we have to make them, and the making requires effort.... But many do not want to make this effort.... By the end of middle age most people have given up the effort.[3]

The capacity to endure change, especially of paradigmatic dimension, is not easily achieved. There may be little enough inducement to expend the energy and time in developing our maps in the first place. In many situations other inducements may be stronger: the demands of a profession, the need to maintain competence in one's employment, the lure of some hobby or pastime. In face of these, strong incentives to examining our faith, with the possible discomfort and inconvenience of changing hard-won positions, might be lacking. Consider the unnerving prospect that such a demanding process might last as long as life itself! Most people may, as Peck suggests, avoid the effort, especially if it is seen as loss of face or weakness to make the changes. Peck acknowledges the power of the natural tendency to avoid change, but also suggests a more fruitful possibility:

> The tendency to avoid challenge is so omnipresent in human beings that it can properly be considered a characteristic of human nature. But calling it natural does not mean it is essential or beneficial or un-

33

changeable behavior.... Indeed, all self-discipline might be defined as teaching ourselves to do the unnatural. Another characteristic of human nature—perhaps the one that makes us most human—is our capacity to do the unnatural, to transcend and hence transform our own nature.[4]

7. To what extent have you experienced the challenge to your "conceptual map" in recent years? Have you been successful in accommodating changes in your theological understanding, or have your beliefs continued essentially unchanged? How do you evaluate the capacity for change in the life of the congregation? How much time is spent in (a) your personal schedule, and (b) in the congregational program, for serious theological discussion? Are there smaller groups devoted to scripture study or other themes among members of the congregation?

8. Though change has also been occurring in the church, it may appear to have been more extensive in our contemporary experience. Perhaps the mere fact that we have been living through it makes it more immediate and unsettling. Do you think there is a limit to the amount of change that can be tolerated over a given period of time? Do you think that limit, if it exists, has been reached?

The Unfinished Task

An abiding hazard for those who take the theological journey seriously is the anxiety or disillusionment that comes with the recognition that there appears to be no end to the process. It is readily understandable why a person should ask: "When will it all end, and what will we be questioning next?" The response is that there is no end, that we cannot predict what element in the tradition, or in our systems, may need to yield to further questioning, and it is not possible to predict the "end." Some issues that at a particular point in time appear formidable may fade in significance, while others may unexpectedly emerge in importance even after they have been considered "settled" and lain dormant for a time. Although the principle of *justification* was established early in the church (Doctrine and Covenants 17:6b) it was not until the 1950s that the concept was revived and began to receive favorable attention. The principle of *grace*, traditionally considered so Protestant that it was never included in any Book of Mormon index, has also been rediscovered and is now understood as the foundational principle on which the gospel rests.[5]

The Basic Beliefs Committee, responsible for the book *Exploring the Faith* (Herald House, 1970), came to the conclusion: "Such a work is never finished because each generation brings its own unique insights and experience to the task."[6] In fact, as one who participated as a member of that committee, I can safely say that even over the lifetime of the committee, different views came to the fore, so that the text as it was published in 1970 differed in some respects from what might have been printed in it a decade earlier. Should a new version of *Exploring the Faith* ever appear, it would again reflect the particular experience and judgments of a subsequent committee. The theological process, and the beliefs that emerge from it, cannot be an undertaking that is done once and then done with, merely to be handed down intact and inviolate to subsequent generations.

The Resistance to New Ideas

New ideas do not come into the world, the church, or even into the life of an individual for that matter, full-blown and immediately accepted and applauded. Such ideas, it has been suggested, generally come into the world as illegitimate and must struggle to earn their legitimacy. It would be extremely difficult to find an exception to this "rule." Nor is it unique or exclusive to the theological process.

In religious groups—and probably in groups of all kinds—antiquity or tradition carries great weight. Ideas or doctrines are sanctified by age, and new ideas are viewed with suspicion if not outright hostility as intruders. In theory it might be easy to accept the view that "the Lord hath yet more light and truth to break forth," but in practice it is another matter. Minuscule ideas, which merely dot the "i"s or cross the "t"s of notions sanctified by time, may be tolerable, but significant ideas will invariably encounter an unsympathetic audience. There can be no absolute guarantee that ideas are valid merely because of their novelty, but neither are they true because of their antiquity.

In this connection, another element exists to make the process hazardous. Because of the high value placed on unity, any exploration of concepts that carry the potential to create division can be seen as apostasy, disrupting the safety of the community. The committee responsible for *Exploring the Faith* had something to say about this matter also:

> A conundrum faces us. How can we allow honest divergence of opinion and still be unified in our faith? The problem has been in our tendency to insist on unity of opinion when it is really in our essential trust in God that we are to be unified. With that fundamental unity we shall be able to establish the mutual confidence and devotion so necessary to working out areas of difference.[7]

The years since the publication of this particular resource have provided a graphic illustration of the value of unity in the faith as interpreted here, and also of the unfortunate fallout that follows our failure to observe the principle that the committee upheld.

The hazards are real. They are not recently arrived on the theological landscape. What I am endeavoring to establish here is the premise that it is not only our faith that requires examination, but also the examiners—that is to say the individuals engaged in the task. The hazards invariably lie with the *subject* (the person engaged in the process) rather than with the *object* (the beliefs being explored).

9. Discuss the suggestion that there is no end to theological reappraisal. Can you think of any time in the history of the church when it might have been desirable to bring the possibility of change to an end? If so, when would that have been and how would the church be different today if that had happened?
10. Suggest any matters that, in your opinion, need to be modified in the near future. These may be among those currently receiving some attention, or others growing out of your own conviction. If you have such suggestions, are they likely to first enter the arena of debate as "illegitimate," or do you anticipate they will receive widespread and instant acclaim?

Activities for the Reader

A. Select a recent issue of the *Saints Herald*. Scan the contents, including editorials, articles, and letters. Adopt the following code, and then make notations in the issue to identify statements or opinions that come under the following categories. Note that more than one code might be applied to the same statement:

    T A traditional concept in Restoration thought

    C A current view or opinion

    D A statement making a strong appeal for a particular idea

    N A critical or negative view of the concept under consideration

What general conclusion can you reach about the content of the issue you have chosen?

B. Select the *oldest* RLDS publication (not including journals or periodicals) and the *newest* publication you have in your library. Then note the following:

- How many years separate the two publications?
- Can you tell, without looking at the date or the appearance of the two, which is the earlier?
- Write a brief statement describing the overall difference between the two.
- Does the date of the more recent book indicate that you have kept up-to-date with current RLDS thought?
- Write down the title and author of the most recent non-RLDS publication you have in your library. Does the general thrust of the book tend to be close to current RLDS thought? If not, make a brief note about any divergences.
- Write a brief statement describing the overall difference of view between the two publications.

Notes

1. Harvey Cox, "Theology: What Is It? Who Does It? How Is It Done?" in *Theologians in Transition*, ed. James M. Wall (New York: Crossroad Press, 1981), 154.
2. James Dittes, "The Christian and Prejudice" in *Ministry* (September 1988).
3. M. Scott Peck. *The Road Less Traveled* (New York: Simon and Schuster, 1978), 44–45.
4. Ibid., 53.
5. The omission of the entry "grace" persists today. It is intriguing to note that the Book of Mormon index moves the reader directly from "gospel" to "grave." (Editor's Note: See *A New Concordance to the Book of Mormon*, Hale and Barbara Lee Collins, compilers [Herald House, 1995] for a list of thirty-one references to "grace" in the Book of Mormon.)
6. Basic Beliefs Committee, *Exploring the Faith* (Independence, Missouri: Herald House, 1970), foreword.
7. Ibid., 245–246.

Theology Preview

Indicate whether you believe each of the following statements to be true or false. The answers will be found on p. 201.

1. The Doctrine and Covenants states that those who are believers, but do not have faith to be healed, should call for the elders of the church for the laying on of hands. T F

2. The church has affirmed its belief in plenary inspiration by conference action. T F

3. The principle of justification by faith means that Christians are justified in following the dictates of their conscience when they have faith. T F

4. The doctrine of the Immaculate Conception is another way of stating the belief that Jesus was born of a virgin. T F

5. The "Epitome of Faith," prepared by Joseph Smith in 1842, was the first authorized statement of belief of the church, and still has official status. T F

6. The church upholds the doctrine of faith healing, which affirms that an individual can expect to be healed of sickness or disease according to the measure of one's faith, or the faith of others on one's behalf. T F

7. The church has approved a formal statement of belief on the resurrection. T F

8. In differences of opinion and matters of debate brought to the World Conference, the correct position is determined by a majority vote of the assembled delegates. T F

9. Eschatology is that branch of theology that deals with the origin of the creation and the life of the earliest inhabitants. T F

39

10. The Book of Mormon is essentially orthodox
    Trinitarian in its view that the Father and the Son
    are not only one in purpose, but are in actuality
    one God.   T   F

Chapter 3

Experience, Language, and Theology

"Theology is thus the primary practical study for those who want to make something of their lives—for those who want to 'get somewhere' worthwhile."

—Arthur Oakman

"Theology is just so many words. I think it is our actual experience with God that is the important thing. We can just get confused with all this talk about theology, but if we depend on our experience then we can't go wrong."

—Sister B to Brother A

There is no doubt that religious experience exerts a formidable impact in the life of the disciple. Recent surveys have concluded that a significant number of Americans report experiences that have had a profound effect on their lives and behavior. This would be similar to reports from previous religious revivals or "awakenings," such as occur approximately every seventy years in American history. Alongside the immediacy and color of experience, theology may seem lifeless and theoretical, as well as being more demanding. "I don't spend time talking about the gospel, I just live it," may appear to many to be the more fruitful way of living out the Christian commitment.

However, the nature of religious experience and the relationship between such experience and theology bear further examination. The following statement by Oakman clearly proposes a significant link between experiencing God and the formulation of concepts about God (theology):

> The ordinary man, we are told, "wants plain, practical religion, not theology." But if he is not a fool, the plain man wants the most accurate ideas possible about God and wants them clearly and simply expressed. This means that the plain man *does* want theology....
>
> Christian experience is always prior to and more fundamental than the creeds. When a man looks at the ocean from the beach, and then goes and looks at a map, he is turning from a contemplation of waves, and sand and sunshine to a bit of colored paper—from something very real to that which is less real. But the map has behind it a massive experience made up by thousands of people who have sailed the seas and chartered the oceans.... And the map is indispensable to those who desire to go across the ocean to other lands....
>
> Of course, studying the map will, of itself, lead nowhere either. Merely learning the Christian doctrines, even gaining the ability to describe and explain them, is less thrilling than walking on the beach or listening to music or smelling flowers. Doctrines and creeds aren't God; they are only a kind of description of how we may find him. Like the map, they point the way and are valuable only to those who *want to go somewhere*. But smelling the flowers and listening to the music is not eternal life either... It may be all thrills and very enjoyable. But to sail our frail bark across "the void of mystery and dread" which looms ahead, we must "take knowledge" of those who have gone before....[1]

It may be helpful to think of theology and experience as being mutually supportive of each other. Theology may help us to gain a better understanding of our experience and the experience of others in similar situations. This may prompt better ways of responding, which in turn opens the way to deeper experience. For example, thoughtful reflection on the meaning and practice of forgiveness may empower a person to express forgiveness in more productive ways. This in turn may open up the way to a deeper experience of the power of forgiveness.

Again, it will make a great deal of practical difference whether people understand Christian love primarily as an emotion or as the intentional and intelligent actions intended for the welfare of another.

The same kind of reciprocal relationship might operate with respect to that dimension of faith referred to as **justification**. The concept was articulated in the first months of the life of the Restoration church (Doctrine and Covenants 17:6b) but virtually ignored, even decried, over the next 125 years. In the absence of thoughtful reflection on the "doctrine," church members essentially were denied the deeper dimensions of the experience conveyed by the concept. The notion that we are justified by faith *alone* (according to Romans 3:28 in the Inspired Version) has only recently returned to our collective consciousness, but has already begun to exert a significant impact in the experience of many members.

1. Review Oakman's comments regarding the practicality of theology cited to this point in the chapter. Do you agree that theology is a "primary practical study" for those who want to get somewhere in life? If so, can you identify situations in your own experience where your specific theological insight or background has served a practical purpose?

2. Roy Cheville was known to comment on some people who wished to live on a "perpetual spiritual high," without appearing able to come down to earth. That is, some desire one "spiritual experience," preferably a spectacular manifestation, after another. If this is so, would it necessarily be a bad thing?

3. It is not uncommon for some Christians to exclude Christian education from their congregational life, preferring that their activities just be "led by the Spirit." Discuss the merits or demerits of this point of view.

Experience Interpreted

The notion may be widespread that whereas theology can run off the rails, experience is completely reliable. "Just trust your experience and you won't go wrong" represents a confidently held view.

However, all experience passes through the filters of our minds and senses. That is to say, our experience is *experience interpreted*, so that the meanings we attach to any occurrence are, in significant degree, a part of who the individual reporting it is. Roy Cheville, formerly a presiding evangelist of the church, wrote of the need to exercise care in the telling of one's experiences:

> Whenever man makes contact with the Divine, he needs to be careful about what he says has happened in him and to him. What he says needs to be restrained by awareness of his limitations about what he knows of God and about what he knows of himself. He does well to distinguish between his firsthand contact with God and his own interpretation of this contact. In the desirable situation they are not separated. Every experience needs to be examined and interpreted soundly. An experience unexamined can be quite dangerous and misused. It is essential that we distinguish between our direct contact with the ocean and our conception of what has happened to us and what the ocean is.[2]

Care and restraint must be exercised in the interpretation of any experience. Further, care must be used to avoid requiring others to accept an interpretation on the basis of feeling "the burning in the bosom" or of having the meaning "given." Without wishing to diminish the significance of any person's reported experience, the practice of the church has been to protect the freedom of each person to evaluate the experience of others as they will, without coercion. As a young district president, I was asked to intervene in a situation where the congregation was considering relocating their building on the existing site. One good elder reported a spiritual experience locating the building in a certain place; another equally fine man reported a spiritual dream locating it elsewhere. The congregation was confused, believing they were obligated to give support to one or the other. The members were advised that they should be respectful of both men, but free to make their decision, uncoerced, according to the best light they had. The building was left where it was and added on to. Obviously this principle of freedom of conscience extends even to documents submitted by the president of the church for consideration by a World Conference. It has been the experience of the church, from time to time, as Cheville pointed out, that unreflected or questionable interpretations have been laid on persons by some who have felt that the acceptance of their experiences (or interpretations) was a mandatory obligation of the Saints.

An admirable instance of sharing an event considered significant by the person reporting it may be found in Russell Ralston's account of his experience during the discussion of the 1984 document brought to the Conference by the president of the church. Elder Ralston requested permission to speak on the document, which proposed the ordination of women, during a meeting of the Quorum of High Priests. His statement concerning his experience, reported in the December 1984 issue of the *Saints Herald,* included the following:

> I have not shared this with others. I have, however, studied it out in my mind and, on numerous occasions, my bosom has burned within me.... I know many in the church have strong feelings in opposition to that which is now revealed.... I do not wish to debate this matter, either for or against, on the basis of what I have heard through the years. I only do that which I believe God asks me to do.... Now that I have presented my testimony, you may accept or reject it. I felt impelled as I enter our meeting this morning to share it. I pray that God will bless us all in our deliberations and discussions concerning this significant matter.[3]

It is obvious that individuals might have conflicting responses to the report of other people's experiences. It is not necessary to go back far in time to recognize that what is inspirational to some will be false to others. Supporters or opponents both might justify their positions by appealing to their own experiences of confirmation or denial. Under such circumstances supporters and detractors might accuse others of absence of the Spirit, lack of intelligence, or impure motives. Such an environment is hardly conducive to genuine dialogue, whether it exists in the course of conference debate or in an adult church school class.

Theology and the Spiritual Gifts

In the tradition of the RLDS Church, a range of experiences or events, generally referred to as "the spiritual gifts," have been accorded great respect. The term has most often been applied to the listing of such gifts by the apostle Paul (I Corinthians 12:7–10) although it is clear that this listing by no means encompasses all experiences that may be regarded as having spiritual significance.

Often members have hoped and looked for those spiritual expressions that might be seen as more spectacular, as if these were the most significant or authoritative. However, the practice of the church has been not to rank gifts in any kind of hierarchy but to allow judgment of all gifts by the fruits that follow. In fact, many years ago, John Garver, then a member of the First Presidency, suggested an arrangement of the Pauline list in Corinthians (Paul does mention other gifts elsewhere) that identified the *primary* gifts as faith, knowledge, wisdom, and discernment. Clearly these would rarely be judged as spectacular, but insofar as they are enduring, rather than episodic, and govern the use of all other gifts, they support Garver's designation. They may also be the ones that are least liable to misuse. That misuse is possible, and has been experienced in the church to the injury and confusion of members, and was the basis of Elbert A. Smith's 1937 articles in the *Saints' Herald* on "Use and Abuse of Spiritual Gifts."[4]

46

It should be noted that these gifts, and others of like kind, are those that facilitate the theological process most effectively. They are not so much single, isolated experiences but have to do with the continuous exercise of reason and scholarship in learning, judgment, and discrimination, rooted in a foundation of faith. Members who engage in theological dialogue should consider and respect experiences reported by individuals, but they are under no obligation to accept a point of view solely on the basis of the claim that it was conveyed in some spiritually spectacular way giving direct access to truth.

It may be true that from time to time a person might sense a breakthrough in a sudden moment of insight and enlightenment—an "Aha!" so to speak. The insights emerging from such moments of illumination may be offered in great sincerity, but they must still stand on their own merits and cannot be imposed on the thinking of the community. As shall be noted in a subsequent chapter, there is no provision in the church for any person to pass infallible judgment on the views of another, no matter what authority and source may be claimed for them. Interpreted experience may be a significant element in the search for truth, but it should not be allowed to override the other gifts and disciplines necessary to the process.

---

3. Do you think that experience can be interpreted incorrectly, as Cheville suggested? Do examples come to mind? What has been the outcome under such conditions? The author suggests that the more spectacular of the spiritual expressions may be most open to misuse. If so, why would this be the case?
4. What positive elements do you identify in Russell Ralston's account of his experience? How would these characteristics contribute to sound theology and enhanced relationships, whatever the subject under discussion?

The Language of Theology

Thus far I have examined the relationship between experience and its interpretation. The thesis was that experience is not necessarily always interpreted accurately and needs to be scrutinized carefully. In a subsequent chapter I will explore some of the factors or influences that have a part in determining how we interpret our experience.

Experience must not only be interpreted, but if it is to be shared with or communicated to others then it must be expressed in language. We now turn to examine the relationship between our experience and the way we express our understanding of that experience in words.

Description of beliefs and discussion of religious matters inevitably involve the use of spoken and written language. Many of the specialized terms used are borrowed from the secular or everyday realm, but invested with a more focused meaning in theological dialogue. Such words as grace, justification, community, redemption, and new life, to name a few, fall into this category. These more common words, along with many that may not be so readily known to us, form the specialized language of theology in much the same way that any branch of knowledge has its own terms.

Theology as Invention

Some may feel the use of a theological vocabulary is pointless, even misleading. They might say: "Why try to change what God has said? After all, we have God's direct words in the scriptures to tell us the truth. All these words that theologians use just complicate the simple truth." This view neglects to acknowledge the church's traditional caution with plenary inspiration, the view that the words of scripture are the directly dictated and precise words of Divinity. The words and phrases used to develop theological statements are *human* terms. There is no celestial dictionary that we can consult to find a list of heaven-given words with clear-cut, precise, and absolute meanings. We make statements that are constructed of human language, put together in such a way as to express our best understandings, and drawn from such resources as are available to us. Indeed, there is a sense in which we may consider theological statements as **invention**. This is not to admit that they are the product of whim or irresponsible fancy, but that the words and phrases used to make such statements are human terms, created by human beings to describe their experience. In this respect, theological language is no different from any other language developed to describe the world about us.

In most cases, however, it is important to be aware that there will be a certain fuzziness around the edges of religious terms. It will generally not be possible for us to specify the one true meaning of such words as faith, love, Spirit, salvation, healing, Zion, or God with such precision that no flexibility is possible. Sometimes people will be using these words and others with at least slightly different meanings, possibly without recognizing what is happening. Should, for example, a resolution be brought to the World Conference inviting delegates to affirm belief in revelation, it is virtually certain that the affirmative vote would be unanimous. However, let the delegates begin to explain more precisely what they mean by "revelation," and several different connotations, some of them widely divergent, would become evident. This fuzziness is not necessarily detrimental, as long as participants realize that there are differences and that they may be talking past each other unless they listen carefully to each other's meanings. The very fuzziness may leave open opportunities for on-going refinement, rather than stifling further exploration by dogmatic edict.

The built-in elasticity of religious terms does, however, raise an ethical principle. Under some circumstances, rather than risk confrontation, people might resort to the use of terms that they know will have a positive emotional impact on their hearers, but privately reserving different meanings for those terms. For example, I might use the word "Zion" in the presence of people whom I know to have a literal understanding of the term, without disclosing the fact that I am using the term in a different, symbolic sense. In this respect, Robert Mesle describes the dilemma:

> This dilemma is not merely one of strategy, but also one of ethics, for it threatens our personal integrity and the integrity of our ministry...we can find ourselves speaking a kind of religious code which evokes approval from our audience while preventing them from understanding our meanings too clearly. We may find ourselves preaching sermons in which our key words and sentences mean one thing to us but another to our congregation.... What if our hearers should discover that our language has meant something very different for us than it meant to them, and that we allowed this to be the case.... Even if they can be made to understand our plight and our good intentions, they feel sorrow that we had so little trust in and regard for them that we were unwilling to share our struggles for new insight.[5]

---

5. Do you think the author's reference to any theological statement as an "invention" is helpful or confusing? Would you have another way of describing the product of thought about matters that ultimately are beyond our capacity to describe in "celestial vocabulary"?

6. How important do you consider it that we make an earnest attempt to describe the meanings in the words we use, even if it highlights differences and raises the possibility of tense feelings? In the class setting, discuss the different meanings members might invest in such terms as Zion, revelation, or spiritual.

Something Lost in the Process

The words of theology are human words, put together to form human statements. They represent the human endeavor to understand and appropriate the revelatory encounter and to lift up the meaning of our experience. Certainly this endeavor cannot be faithfully undertaken without utilization of the gifts with which our lives are graced. Faith, insight, discernment, and reason are crucial, as well as the mutual help we extend to each other, and the disciplines of prayer, fasting, meditation, and study. Nevertheless, we must confess that our best insights reflect not only our partial comprehension, but also the inadequacy of our language.

The view is sometimes expressed that if God is the author of some communicated intelligence, either through scripture or other "direct" means, then the language must be flawless, and we will be exposed to absolute truth, as opposed to "mere" human thoughts:

> Some may say, "Theology is conditional and relative, and that is precisely why I have nothing to do with it. I prefer the knowledge of God to the knowledge of men." Involved here is an understanding of revelation that speaks in terms of revealed doctrine. That is to say, God himself dictates doctrinal formulations and information for us to learn and repeat. Revelation is understood in terms of words from God, thereby giving us a divinely dictated theology... The assumption is, of course, that information received directly from God is naturally to be preferred to anything we might try to figure out for ourselves on the basis of our finite reason alone.[6]

As appealing as this argument might sound, it makes or imposes an unreal expectation on the language we use. For this reason Arthur Oakman has stated (as cited in chapter 1) that "strictly speaking, there are no revealed truths." The following statement elaborates Oakman's thought, describing the loss that takes place when experience is translated into language:

> Once experience with God is sustained, certain truths about the experience may be distilled from it.... It has been my contention that revelation is actually always more than our apprehension or record of it.... The treasure is held in earthen vessels, but the vessels in which it is held are and remain human.... When the word of God is trans-

posed into a word of man, there is always something of infinite value lost in the process.[7]

It was this same point of view that F. Henry Edwards expressed many years ago in his ground-breaking book, *Fundamentals*:

> Revelation, then, is one thing, and the record of revelation is another..... To record the truth thus received has involved the almost insurmountable problem of injecting spiritual significance into words which have become heavy and soiled in the commonplace traffic of human experience.[8]

This honest confession is not to belittle or negate the importance of the words, whether those words appear in scripture or in the statements of doctrine of the church or in the preached word. But it does remind us that the authority of the words does not reside in their perfection or infallibility but in their power to serve as a vehicle for the experience of the revelation in our own time and in our own experience.

Roy Cheville has also pointed to the relationship between experience of the ultimate and the terms in which such experience, as understood, may be rendered:

> In religion men try to speak about spiritual reality that is far beyond their comprehension. They use their own figures of speech and rituals to indicate what they have in mind and heart. These are instruments for their religious expressions; they are not the inclusive reality.[9]

Although Joseph Smith III, giving evidence in the Temple Lot Suit, had stated that the church did not subscribe to the idea of "plenary inspiration," the church (in GCR 308) adopted a more conservative position, content to say that the doctrine was "not affirmed," which is somewhat different from being "denied." However, we are left with the situation that even if such an instance of "direct" revelation should occur there could be no infallible authority to affirm the fact that it was, indeed, infallible. All such occurrences rest with the judgment of fallible judges.

Thus the words of theology are not the reality, though hopefully they point to the reality and constitute a vehicle whereby we may come in touch with the reality. The treasure *is* in earthen vessels. There is no description of God, even given the tongues of angels (whatever that might mean), that encompasses God, nor is any formulated statement of love equal to the reality. Something of value *is* lost in the process. Sacred writings and the formulated statements of doctrine are neither the substance nor the reality of revelation. We use the language available to us to share our experience as best we can, aware of its inadequacies, but also assured that such language may be the means of insight, understanding, and renewed life.

In acknowledging the inadequacies and pitfalls of using human language, we may nevertheless appreciate its potential usefulness and power, and develop discipline in using words as accurately and descriptively as possible. Without the language of theology there can be no speaking about the faith, no witness, no declaration of the gospel, no prayer, teaching, or worship. But it is always well to remember that theology is not itself faith; it is the product of faith and an invitation to faith.

7. Discuss the idea that expressing truth in human language is like holding "treasure in earthen vessels"? Do you ever feel fully satisfied with your ability to express or share your beliefs? Are there other factors underlying your convictions that are just as strong or stronger than the language you use to express them?

8. In what way can we think of theology as an invitation to faith? How has your own theological journey strengthened your faith? Does the fact that your theological journey may be unfinished discourage you?

Activities for the Reader

A. For one week, record any religious terms whose meaning might be unfamiliar to you. Consult a dictionary or religious text to determine the meaning of these terms and make a record of your information. If you do not encounter any unknown words identify some with which you are more or less familiar and follow the same procedure.

B. Follow up any questions related to the theology preview which preceded this chapter, doing whatever research is within your reach. Make notes on two or three of these items for your reference.

Notes

1. Arthur A. Oakman, "Theology, Its Place and Meaning," *Saints' Herald* 113, no. 9 (May 1, 1966): 294ff.
2. Roy Cheville, *Scriptures from Ancient America* (Independence, Missouri: Herald House, 1964), 26.
3. Russell Ralston, "Led By the Spirit," *Saints' Herald* 131, no. 23 (December 1984): 549.
4. Elbert A. Smith, "Use and Abuse of Spiritual Gifts," *Saints' Herald* 84, nos. 46 and 47 (November 13 and 20, 1937).
5. Robert Mesle, "The Ethics of Religious Language," *Commission* (April 1985): 10.
6. Verne Sparkes, *The Theological Enterprise* (Independence, Missouri: Herald House, 1969), 30.
7. Arthur Oakman, "Treasure in Earthen Vessels," *Saints' Herald* 114, no. 11 (June 1, 1967): 6–7.
8. F. Henry Edwards, *Fundamentals* (Independence, Missouri: Herald House, 1948), 256.
9. Cheville. *Scriptures From Ancient America*, 17.

Chapter 4

Belief, Faith, and Creed

**"There lives more faith in honest doubt,
Believe me, than in half the creeds."**
—Alfred, Lord Tennyson, "In Memoriam"

"*Credo ut intelligam*—I believe in order that I might understand."
—St. Augustine

"You just have to have faith; the church tells us what to believe, and that's good enough for me."
—Father to son

Theology is the natural outcome of the conviction that we are called to live out the gospel in the life of the world. H. Grady Davis describes the gospel in the following terms:

The Gospel is the news of God's redemptive action in Jesus Christ our Lord, revealing God's love toward [us] and purpose in history, manifesting at once God's judgment and mercy, furnishing a new basis for the relationship between us and God—compassion, forgiveness, unmerited favor and help—and calling into being a reconstituted humanity joined with Christ and living no longer by its biological possibilities, but by participation in Christ's life.[1]

Obviously the good news of this event must be communicated. The implicit danger is that the words used to interpret and communicate the event are substituted for the event itself, so that the gospel is thought of as a set of propositions or principles. Thus the commentary on the event rather than the event itself might be thought of as constituting the essence of the gospel. In this context, the "fullness of the gospel"—a phrase that has been familiar to members of the RLDS Church—has sometimes been understood as a complete and superior set of teachings relating to doctrine, church organization, etc. contained in the scriptural resources of the church. The risks in such a view are apparent. Propositions (doctrines) may explicate or interpret the gospel, but they are not themselves the gospel, described as "the glad tidings which the voice out of the heavens bore unto us, that he came into the world, even Jesus to be crucified for the world, and to bear the sins of the world... (Doctrine and Covenants 76:4g).

Faith Is Central

Central to the life in Christ is the response of faith. If "the just shall live by faith" (Romans 1:17)—a statement that itself illustrates the need for interpretation of biblical statements—then faith is at the heart of the journey. Faith has often been understood as a belief in and acceptance of the right doctrines, so that a person who might question certain teachings could be accused of being "weak in the faith."

It is informative to see what happened to the notion of faith in the early centuries of the church. In the Gospels and the letters of Paul faith is essentially understood as a relationship of trust and commitment to Christ. However, toward the end of the century, faith was beginning to refer more to acceptance of a body of teachings. The disciples were advised to "earnestly contend for the faith which was once delivered to the saints" (Jude 3). As the hierarchical structure of the church became the basis of authority and the need to resist heresy intensified, "faith" was increasingly interpreted as the obligation to defer and assent to the rulings of those in authority:

56

You should all follow the bishop as Jesus Christ did the Father. Follow, too, the presbytry as you would the apostles; and respect the deacons as you would God's law. Nobody must do anything that has to do with the Church without the bishop's approval.... [W]hatever he approves pleases God as well. In that way everything you do will be on the safe side and valid.[2]

It is unfortunate that the circumstances prevailing during the precarious years of the church's early existence encouraged the emphasis on assent rather than confident trust. As the church became increasingly authoritative, the punishment for dissent became increasingly severe. It may be noted in passing that although the formal processes of the inquisition of earlier centuries no longer exist, Christians still often judge each other's "faithfulness" by their orthodoxy of belief and can be just as cruel in their treatment of those found wanting.

---

1. Discuss the various ways to understand the term "fullness of the gospel." With which meanings were you familiar in earlier years, or as you grew up in the church? Has there been a significant change in the way members interpret the term "gospel"? If so, what effect has this change had in practical terms on the ministry of the church?
2. Discuss the principle of faith as described above and as members of the class understand it. Keeping in mind that theology is a practical exercise and should have a practical impact on the conduct of our lives, what is the difference between "justification by faith" and "justification by works"?

Rethinking Faith

The notion that faith requires a person to give assent and support to a body of authoritative teachings still prevails among Christians. In some faith communities such assent is the hallmark of acceptability. Failure to exhibit such assent may bring recrimination, either official or informal. There does appear to be evidence that in the prevailing religious climate, at least in the United States, churches or groups that require unquestioning assent to "authoritative" tenets are experiencing the most rapid growth. In times of social change and anxiety many people may welcome such external authoritative guidance.

Whatever merit there may be in such a life-pattern, biblical faith calls us beyond assent. Faith does not have to do primarily with assent to doctrines but with trust in and commitment to God in Christ. Such a disposition will, of course, issue in the profession of ideas or doctrines (by the process of theologizing), but correctness of doctrine, which must always be relative, is hardly the test of faith. Arthur Oakman, despite a healthy respect for and commitment to learning, drew an important distinction between certainty (that is, knowing correct doctrines) and assurance (experiencing a trusting relationship): "Faith is decision, not conclusion. Christianity is not a form of knowledge, nor is it a matter of holding correct doctrines.... Faith is a relationship of trust, not a system of belief about God."[3]

The relationship described above, however, finds expression in statements of belief, or, in the more formal sense, doctrines. On occasion it has been suggested that all one needs to have is "simple" faith, as if the absence of reason and thought justified a feeling called "faith." Such a point of view is sometimes advanced as an excuse for not undertaking the more demanding discipline of developing a reasoned faith. However, the point of view advanced in Doctrine and Covenants 85:36a links faith and reason in a necessary relationship, not as alternate paths to wisdom. In his book *Fire in My Bones* Robert Mesle explores the spirit and character of faith, describing a lifestyle that manifests both an affirmative and trusting commitment and a serious investment in the discipline of reason:

Faith is not a license to believe whatever we wish about Christ. It is rather a commitment which drives us to seek the best available understanding of Christ in terms of what we can honestly know about history, scripture, the nature of revelatory experience, and the nature of the world in general.[4]

It would be difficult indeed to visualize or conceive of faith without beliefs of some kind, consciously developed or otherwise. On the other hand, it is possible that beliefs or doctrines can be held, even tenaciously, without the relationship of trusting commitment described by Oakman as faith. In describing the relationship between faith and belief Augustine, bishop of Hippo (354–430), a theologian of the first order, held that faith *preceded* and paved the way for understanding. The quality of faith would rescue theology from the dry bones of intellectual curiosity or reason alone, so that belief then emerged as more than an academic exercise. Under these circumstances, thoughtful Christians were then better able to "give a quiet and reverent answer" to account for the presence of their faith.

3. How do you respond to Oakman's assertion that faith is not primarily a system of belief about God but a relationship of trust? Do you find this confirmed in your own life and experience? In what sense is faith a matter of decision rather than conclusion? Can you recall occasions in your life when faith has involved decision?

4. Relating what you know about "justification" and "faith," how do you interpret the statement in Romans 1:17 that "The just shall live by faith," or as the RSV states it: "He who through faith is righteous shall live."

Inquiring Faith[5]

A healthy skepticism, rooted in trust, is no threat to faith but rather a necessary outcome and preserver of faith. Doubt is hardly the opposite of faith, as has sometimes been claimed, especially by those whose own dogmatic views might have been opened to scrutiny. Such a healthy skepticism is far more fruitful than the naive or unthinking acceptance that often passes for faith. It is not uncommon that such a superficial belief system, when subjected to the realities of life, will be tested and found wanting. The failure of such "faith" to stand the test of time and experience frequently will result in disillusionment and skepticism toward all religious values—a phenomenon sometimes referred to as "throwing out the baby with the bathwater."

It must be admitted that there are risks associated with the venture of inquiring doubt or, as Christopher Morse has defined it, "faithful disbelief."[6] Nevertheless, the risks associated with avoiding the process are greater:

> Our failure to challenge our own faith, even to its deepest roots, has at least two very nasty results. First, we fail to discover which aspects of our faith are flawed, inaccurate, incomplete, or just plain wrong. That's the good news. The bad news is, that we also fail to discover which aspects of our faith are valid, are dependable, and will carry much more weight than *we* will otherwise trust to them. We can't find the things that are valuable without the risk of finding those that are not.[7]

To keep to the path of inquiring doubt (or inquiring faith, to use Paul Edwards's term), to ask the hard questions, will rarely be a tranquil and untroubled journey. Yet, as Arthur Oakman has insisted, it is the questions rather than the answers that enhance spiritual power and intellectual stature. This is not to suggest that the attitude of faithful doubt leaves all questions in a state of perpetual suspension, with no decisions made and no actions taken. Nevertheless, insofar as answers may potentially (though not necessarily) close off further inquiry, there is a timely warning couched in the saying, "Knowledge is the tombstone for search."

5. Do you see yourself in a position of "faithful disbelief?" If so, with what concern or questions is your
   disbelief engaged? Are others in your congregation
   aware of your struggle, and if so, how do they feel
   about it? Do you have "fellow-travelers," either in
   the congregation or elsewhere, with whom you can
   share your disbelieving?

The Resistance to Creed-making

A creed may be understood as a set of fundamental beliefs,
sometimes accorded official authority by some kind of formal
action, but perhaps established by the informal processes of
time and tradition. The RLDS Church, while producing informal statements of belief from time to time, has never authorized a comprehensive formal statement of belief intended to
serve as a binding formula. Periodically statements have been
published, either over the signature of individuals or as the
work of a committee, that were intended to be advisory in nature. What has come to be described as the "Epitome of Faith,"
prepared by Joseph Smith Jr., would fall into this category. This
statement, like others, may have been inaccurately interpreted
by some members as bearing formal authority. However, although members may be inclined to assert, in the course of a
theological discussion, that "the church believes..." it is in fact
that the church has rarely approved statements of belief concerning faith or doctrine. Two rare exceptions are GCR 391 (in
1894, concerning the resurrection) and GCR 783 (in 1918, subsequently rescinded).

This may be illustrated with a reference to baptism. From
time to time conferences of the church, essentially guided by
interpretations of statements from the Three Standard Books,
have specified requirements for the mode of baptism (immer-
sion), the minimum age of candidates (eight years), the min-

isterial office of officiating ministers (priests or elders), and the baptismal formula. A broad statement concerning fitness for baptism has also served as a general guideline (Doctrine and Covenants 17:7). However, no formal statement of the meaning and purpose of baptism has been authorized, though general references to entry into the body of Christ, remission of sins, and newness of life tend to be cited most often.

Other matters of belief may be even less specifically defined. Although there is no shortage of written material about God, such data carries no World Conference or other similar binding sanction, and is intended as helpful resource material for interested individuals. The range of opinion and expression among church members and leaders is quite broad, as might be expected. When a number of years ago the *Herald* carried articles by a member of the Quorum of Twelve (Arthur A. Oakman, July 6, 1953) and the presiding evangelist (Elbert A. Smith, August 10, 1953) reflecting radically different views of the Godhead, many members were disturbed. Indeed, this situation had some effect in discontinuing the inclusion in the *Herald* of the feature titled "Department for Debatable Topics." This was not because the topic of God was not debatable. Rather, the very use of such a title carried the erroneous implication that positions stated in other parts of the *Herald* were somehow officially sanctioned and not debatable. This was not the case. Unless specifically designated as "official," all statements and views stand on their own merits.

The absence of an authoritative creedal statement has been troublesome to some members. A number of years ago the following question appeared in the Question Time feature of the *Herald*, probably reflecting a concern held by more than the one inquirer: "Why doesn't the church codify its beliefs so that ordinary members with limited theological background can answer with certainty? One question in my mind is that of the Godhead. Is there an official position on the 'trinity' or the 'unity' concepts?"

In his response church historian Charles Davies cited a celebrated article by President Israel A. Smith in the February 1, 1954, issue of the *Herald*, titled "The Godhead, Dogma and the 'Iron Bedstead.'" Although President Smith cited some previous statements concerning the nature of the Godhead, he doubted the propriety of searching too energetically for dogmatic conclusions, suggesting that there was

"a desire on the part of some members to secure from the First Presidency *ex cathedra* opinions as to controverted matters, apparently with the idea of getting the church committed on immaterial questions."... Then the late president of the church went on to say, "We must admit that the question of the Godhead is a difficult one. However, there is no doctrine of salvation involved. I am sure nobody is going to be disciplined by Divinity or denied salvation for resolving it wrongly. It is one among possibly hundreds of theological questions wherein one will not become a heretic however wrong he may be."[8]

The principles implied in this exchange give rise to some intriguing questions. Would an authoritative interpretation from the First Presidency, or any other body, provide the ordinary member with any degree of certainty? Upon what questions may a person be judged a heretic, if any? Are there, in effect, some tests of faith, matters on which the "correct" answer is necessary for faithful membership, or for the right to be authorized as an ordained minister? If so, who is to determine such questions? How does one decide whether a particular question is immaterial or not? Reports in the public media from time to time commenting on "heresy trials" in some religious bodies highlight the pitfalls associated with the attempt to judge matters of faith by formal tribunals.

As early as 1879 (GCR 222) the General Conference had cautioned against actions that, under the claim to liberty of conscience, could do violence to "the honesty and integrity of the people by prescribing dogmas and tenets other than the plain provisions of the gospel." However, neither at that time nor at any time subsequently has action been taken to specify precisely what those "plain provisions" were. It would appear that in this matter, as in many others, it is the "spirit" rather than the "letter" that should be observed.

The caution of the church regarding dogmatic pronouncements or decisions claiming infallibility was clearly and aptly pointed out by Joseph Smith III in the course of giving evidence in the Temple Lot Suit:

> So far as our action or allegiance to any rule of doctrine of faith or practice is concerned, so far as anything comes to us, and is accepted by the church, as a rule for its guidance either in faith or practice the matter of fallibility or infallibility does not enter into the question. There is no tribunal this side of the judgment seat of God that can determine whether anything is true or not true absolutely; but when anything is accepted, of course it is binding upon the church, although we do not attempt to pass upon the question of its fallibility or infallibility. We simply decide these matters according to the light that is given to us, and we are liable to be in error, for we recognize that this side of the judgment seat there is no tribunal that can decide that matter.[9]

6. Do you believe the church is too lax in allowing a wide range of belief and that some items of belief should be required for faithful membership? If so, what would these be?
7. As noted above, GCR 222 affirmed the importance of giving recognition to "the plain provisions of the gospel." In the absence of any identification of such provisions, what do you think these might be? To what extent do you believe it would be possible to achieve agreement on these provisions, or upon the interpretation of their meaning?

It should be clear, then, that pronouncements on matters of faith and doctrine, even those issued by authoritative bodies, are matters of opinion, albeit informed opinion, and should not claim final or absolute authority. Statements may be made, decisions agreed upon, and positions given support, but still with the recognition that while made with the best understanding available and with such guidance of the Holy Spirit as may be felt, they cannot claim infallibility or be imposed with the force of dogma.

Why has such a stance been the tradition of the church? Does it imply that members do not believe much, or do not believe strongly? Certainly not. The reasons are either stated directly or implied in a report to the Conference of 1885 that appeared in the *Saints' Herald*:

> The attempt to force the church into the declaration of a formulated creed failed as heretofore. There was no disposition to build the "iron bedstead" upon which to stretch the devotee. It was equally apparent that the body had little sympathy with any effort to destroy the integrity of the revelations of God to the church. It was considered that to declare upon this point at the demand of one, involved the precedent to declare upon another point at the demand of someone else; and if for these, then at the requirement of any who chose to rise up and demand a declaration of dogma, the church would have to yield, the result of which would be to finally eliminate the liberty of individual inquiry, quench the teaching of the word of God, and practically deny the office work of the Spirit in leading unto truth. Once involved in the intricacies of such formulated declarations there could be no abiding lines of demarcation where belief might safely rest and dogmatism assume the rule. It was and is far safer to affirm the books of the church, as with one so with the other, than to build a creed.[10]

An Abiding Principle

This hesitancy, even resistance, to formalizing statements of faith may be illustrated, not only from early situations but from more recent occasions. In 1962 the World Conference declined to act on the question of the virgin birth. In 1986 a resolution requiring the church to adopt a specific view on the translation of the Book of Mormon was declared out of order by the presiding officer, and his ruling was upheld by the Conference. These actions did not necessarily signify disbelief in these matters but rather a hesitancy to act dogmatically on them, and a recognition of the difficulties that would inevitably follow upon such dogmatically stated positions. Conference decisions or judgments from properly authorized bodies more appropriately deal with procedures, as in the case of the sacraments, or the process for calling individuals to the priesthood, thereby providing a level of consistency in directing the affairs of the church.

There have been some exceptions, though only a few, to the position regarding dogmatic statements on matters of faith or doctrine. One such instance (mentioned earlier in this chapter) which is informative for the circumstances surrounding it, occurred in 1894, in response to a request from the membership for an official statement from the First Presidency:

> The Presidency to whom the subject of the resolution was referred, report: That, while we are of the opinion that the standard books of the church clearly teach the unconditional resurrection of man, we believe it to be of doubtful propriety for the church to put unnecessary restrictions upon the ministry as to the manner of their teaching those doctrines and matters of faith which are of secondary importance, for, while possible injury may accrue to individuals, here and there, who may be inquiring for the word, from the advocacy of individual views held by some of the laborers in the field; we think such injury less hurtful to the general work than that which would result from the creation of a creed, or putting restrictions upon the ministry in the form of resolutions restraining the liberty of inquiry and investigation and censuring those who may venture into such investigation upon what seems to them to be fair grounds. We therefore recommend that the Conference go no further than to say that it is the belief of the church that the doctrine of the resurrection provides for the rising from the dead of all men, each in his own order, through the atonement wrought by Jesus Christ.[11]

It will be noted that the operative part of the resolution is extremely brief, fewer than thirty words. It is questionable whether it would have satisfied many of those desiring a more detailed position. The Presidency then appended a selection of eighteen passages of scripture from the Bible, Book of Mormon, and Doctrine and Covenants with the expressed hope that such passages "may be aids to understanding upon the subject." Clearly the intention was that members should accept responsibility and initiative in searching the resources, without yielding to the desire for officially conveyed statements. In may be concluded that the prefatory statement, regarding creedal statements in general, was considerably more significant than the actual statement on the resurrection itself.

The tradition of the church has been to encourage the active, disciplined search for truth as a natural expression of one's discipleship. We live in a time when many, shrinking from the complexities of the modern world, seek simple, unambiguous answers from authority figures. Under these circumstances, individuals lose the will and capacity to process information or to look within themselves to harness the resources for discovering meanings. The Reorganization, resisting the lure of simple, unreflected thought, upholds the challenge for serious theological dialogue, both as a personal stewardship and between individuals.

Our Creed—All Truth

From the early years of the church it has been customary to cite the phrase, "Our creed—all truth," when pressed to give an explanation of our noncreedal position. This has itself been subject to differing interpretations. There have been times when some have acted as if it meant "We know everything that is true" or "Everything that we know is true," and have acted in ways consistent with their belief. Perhaps somewhat less ambitious, yet nevertheless courageous, has been the claim: "Everything that is true that is worth knowing, we know." Often it has been interpreted to mean: "Nobody but us can possess any real truth," or a little less presumptuous, "We possess more truth than anybody else."

While it might have been ignored frequently, the traditional modesty of the church with respect to truth would probably claim that the most faithful interpretation of "Our creed—all truth" is: "We shall appreciate truth wherever it is to be found," and again, "Recognizing our finitude and fallibility, we shall continue the search for truth." Such an attitude is most conducive to the theological task.

8. Review the several suggested interpretations of the statement, "Our creed—all truth." Which of these do you prefer, or do you recommend a better statement still? Discuss some of the difficulties associated with the interpretations other than your preference.

The tradition and practice of the church in relation to the expression of its beliefs have been fruitful, even though some have been uncomfortable with the apparent weakness of a noncreedal position. The Saints have been provided with resources for personal and corporate study, but at the same time have been encouraged to accept personal responsibility for establishing their structure of belief. Inquiring faith holds the promise of disciplined theology and mature discipleship.

9. The pronounced tradition of the church, reflected in Conference resolutions and other statements, has been that differences of opinion should be valued, so long as they are held in a good spirit. How successfully do you think this position has been honored? How do you feel when individuals, perhaps including those in positions of significant leadership, express differing opinions?

Activities for the Reader

A. Select one belief you consider to be of primary importance. Then write a brief paragraph expressing your thoughts about this belief. You may wish to consult one or more references, such as the book *Exploring the Faith* (Herald House, 1970; revised by Alan Tyree, 1987) for some assistance, but as far as possible the statement should be your own product.

B. Write down two or three matters of belief for which you may currently hold "faithful disbelief." For each one, specify a person, or a printed resource that you could consult in working through your questions. If you follow this through, make notes of what your resources suggested.

Notes

1. H. Grady Davis, *Design for Preaching* (Philadelphia: Fortress Press, 1958), 109.
2. Letter of Ignatius, Bishop of Antioch, to the Smyrnaeans (about A.D. 110), 8:1–2. Translation from *Early Christian Fathers*, ed. Cyril C. Richardson (New York: Macmillan, 1970).
3. Arthur Oakman, "The Spirit of a Sound Mind," *Saints' Herald* 114, no. 16 (August 15, 1967): 13.
4. Robert Mesle, *Fire in My Bones* (Independence, Missouri: Herald House, 1984), 151.
5. I have borrowed this term from the title of the book by Paul M. Edwards, *Inquiring Faith: An Exploration in Religious Education* (Independence, Missouri: Herald House, 1967).
6. Christopher Morse, *Not Every Spirit: A Dogmatics of Christian Disbelief* (Valley Forge, Pennsylvania: Trinity Press International, 1994).
7. I believe that this point of view, expressed by church member friend Art Palmer in the course of a recent conversation, is worth preserving.
8. Charles Davies, *Question Time*, Volume 2 (Independence, Missouri: Herald House, 1967):10–12.
9. Abstract of Evidence, Temple Lot Suit, 1893, sections 158, 161, 162: 492–494.
10. *Church History* (1885), 4:484.
11. General Conference Resolution 391 (1894).

Chapter 5

Sources and Lenses

"My servants of the leading quorums are commended for their diligence in seeking more light and truth from all available sources. For have I not told you that my glory is intelligence and he that seeketh learning by study and by faith will be rewarded in this life and the life to come."
—Doctrine and Covenants 149:5

"Our faith is founded on revelation. I was taught the church's beliefs at my mother's knee and that is sufficient. Besides that, the simple message of the scriptures provides us with the perfect guide."
—Heard at a Wednesday evening fellowship service

Clearly, those engaged in the theological enterprise are concerned with the search for and discovery of truth. To refer to a slogan associated with a publication whose credibility might not be of the highest order: "Inquiring minds want to know." This raises the question of **epistemology**, the study of the nature and grounds of knowledge, especially with reference to its limits and validity. In terms of our beliefs, the simple form of the question might be: "How do we know what we claim to know?" Related to this is the question: "Are there limits to what we can know?" Because belief claims to rest on reliable

71

knowledge, it will be important to explore how such knowledge is acquired and how authoritative it can be.

Several important questions immediately arise. In the first place, are there different ways we may speak of "knowing" something? Consider the *quantitative* element of knowledge: its degree of public confirmation or empirical evidence to establish its reliability. In this sense I can "know" that the church was established on April 6, 1830, because I judge the verifiable facts to be well established. Further, I may feel safe in assuming that all people conversant with the facts are in agreement. However, in many matters—especially including matters on which individuals place a high degree of value—we may use the word "know" in a different sense. I may, for example, say: "I know that I can trust my wife," or "I know that my friend will be dependable." In these instances my "knowledge" rests predominantly on convictions that are more difficult to verify by public data. Others may reach different conclusions; what they claim to "know" might well be different from the "knowledge" I have expressed.

There may, then, be degrees of conviction depending on the reliability of the witnesses and the interpretation of available data. In fact, people present at and witnessing the same events (or are they the *same* events?) may recall them differently, or interpret what was taking place in different ways. Reality, for each of us, will be influenced significantly by who we are and what we "see." Thus interpretation of what has "happened" at a World Conference will be deeply shaped by the point of view we have invested in matters under consideration. I have been present at Conferences where some have insisted that the presiding officers "leaned over backwards" to give opportunity for opposing points of view to be heard, while others adamantly claimed that these same officers had ridden roughshod over those known to have dissenting views. So firmly persuaded are both "sides" of the legitimacy of their interpretations that they can scarcely credit with integrity others who differ. So extensively are we influenced by such kinds of "knowledge" that it may be said that people inhabit different worlds, or conduct their lives from different worldviews.

The Gateway to Meaning

In examining our religious convictions, then, we will be aware that there is a kind of knowing that is not totally and perhaps not even significantly dependent on the evidence of public opinion or of our senses. There will be a *qualitative* dimension to our experience having to do with the intensity or persuasiveness of events that defy rational explanation. In this respect Donald Walhout has written:

> The gateway to religious truth is to be found in those peculiarly intimate and incisive experiences called, in the philosophical sense, intuitive, and in the religious sense, revelatory. Religion does not live and move on the plane of sensory observation or rational analysis but in the dimension of experience we have delineated as personal awareness or...personal encounter.[1]

Almost without exception people will deeply value such experiences, the meaning they impute to them in the formation of their faith, and the accompanying beliefs that spring from them. Experiences to which people have attached revelatory significance will be cited as highly authoritative in theological discussion. In the Restoration tradition it has been customary to describe such mystical events as "a burning in the bosom," being "given to know," or being addressed by the Spirit. Of course, it will be evident that such revelatory experiences may occur in a number of ways, including the quiet, gradual, and unspectacular growth of understanding which opens the way to new insights. If fact, if we are honest, we will acknowledge that although remarkable "revelatory" insights may have occurred from time to time (at least as we have interpreted or evaluated such events), the greater part of our belief system has developed in quiet and gradual ways, "line upon line, precept upon precept." On the other hand, evidence

73

appears to be lacking that those who claim frequent experiences of spectacular character are noticeably better informed or more mature in their theological understandings.

There have been occasions when people felt that certain kinds of experience, such as those more spectacular kinds specified above, were necessarily superior ways of delivering truth with absolute and unquestionable certainty. As suggested in an earlier chapter, this is not consistent with the tradition and practice of the church. Experience itself, no matter how persuasive to the individual, might be misinterpreted. Accordingly, other lenses, or gateways to truth, are appropriate:

> To know God involves faith, revelation, and reason. Revelation does not seem ever to be in the form of utter and complete proof. It is sustained by faith, critically appreciated by reason, and thus is a continuing process in the lives of the committed. God never overrides human intelligence making men believe or know what they cannot encompass.[2]

Thus intelligence and reason are not impediments to revelation, but are rather the necessary means through which the revelatory encounter is appreciated and interpreted. Here the element or discipline of reason is added as an integral part of theological exploration and dialogue. Although sometimes the rational factor may be belittled as "mere reason" it surely must be poor reasoning that is to be guarded against rather than reason *per se*. To be more specific, one of the better known references in the Doctrine and Covenants identifies reason as a necessary precursor and test of the revelatory experience. Illumination comes when the discipline of reason has been called into play, to guard against untested naïveté or simple credulity:

> Behold, you [Oliver Cowdery] have not understood; you have supposed that I would give it unto you, when you took no thought, save it was to ask me; but, behold, I say unto you, that you must study it out in your mind; then you must ask me if it be right, and if it is right,

I will cause that your bosom shall burn within you; therefore, you shall feel that it is right.[3]

To draw a sharp distinction between the rational and the intuitive, and to claim that the solid rock of revelation is preferable to the shifting sands of human reason, is to ignore the truth that all our "fallen" faculties participate in the response to revelation. We cannot claim that intelligence and reason are defective, whereas perception and intuitive grasp are infallible. This is surely one reason why the church has not been disposed to grant the status of infallibility to any means of discovery. It is also to ignore the fact that revelation may be experienced just as significantly through the exercise of thought, study, and reason ("studying it out in the mind") as it may be through other "mystical" means.

1. Refer to the statement by Arthur Oakman relating the processes of revelation, faith, and reason as avenues to truth. Have you experienced events in which revelation, faith, and reason appeared to function in a significant relationship? What was the outcome in terms of what you came to understand?
2. On occasion individuals have been heard to say when defending some viewpoint or conclusion they have reached: "I couldn't have reasoned this out or known it of my own ability, so it has to be God who enlightened me." Evaluate this statement.

Many Paths to Truth

In addition to those sources mentioned above, individuals will appeal to other sources of authority, consciously or otherwise. In all probability, most people depend on several sources, though often one will predominate. Each individual will need to be aware of how these sources influence his or her thinking and be free to evaluate the validity of these several elements on any specific issue. Consider the following:

It's in the scriptures (the appeal to scripture). Latter Day Saints traditionally have made a strong appeal to the authority of scripture. Methods of scriptural interpretation will vary from time to time, and recent generations might not place as much reliance in passages prized by their predecessors. For example, interpretation of prophecies, so important to earlier generations, appears to hold little interest for contemporary church members or to feature prominently in missionary witnessing to friends. More detailed attention will be given to scripture as a source for theology in chapter 6.

Our church says so (the appeal to institutional authority). Although the church has acted formally on matters of faith much less frequently than generally supposed, members may sometimes assume that their positions or opinions are indeed sustained by official pronouncements or decisions. In many cases, it would be more accurate to say "Most people say so," or even "It's my opinion, and I assume that the church agrees." In most instances, if an appeal to the institution is to be made, it would be more accurate to cite a predominant opinion among members, if such could be determined, but this should be recognized for what it is.

We've always believed it (the appeal to tradition). This may be true in many instances, though not as often as might be suspected. People often assume that what they have heard during their lifetime in the church must always have been believed. Members may witness females routinely voting in legislative sessions without realizing that before 1867 this was not the case. Before that time, most members did not believe that women had the right to vote, and indeed many members opposed the view after 1867 when the matter was reversed by Conference vote. By the same token, the weight of tradition varies from region to region. What might be accorded authority on the basis of tradition in one part of the church (even in one congregation) might not enjoy the same reputation in another part.

Further, the faith may be illuminated or distorted by our particular history as a denomination. It is tempting to take our current meanings and read them back into our history. For many years around the opening of the twentieth century the interpretation of biblical statements and (purported) history to "prove" that the Christian church went into apostasy in A.D. 570 was common wisdom for members of the Reorganization. Beginning with the year 1830, we worked back 1260 years (a figure derived from scriptural references) to conclude that an apostasy began in 570 and lasted until the Restoration.[4] Although the "facts" thus invoked bore little relation to reality, they constituted the reality with which church members lived. In the same fashion the way we read the New Testament resulted in the creation in our minds of a system of "priesthood" which bore little resemblance to what we now know to have been the reality. The temptation was to select supposed "facts" and press them into a pattern that justified the conclusions established that we had come to believe. Here again, the responsible exercise of scholarship in studying the earliest post-New Testament writings has helped us to be more faithful to history.

Joseph Smith said so (the appeal to founding authority). Although the founding prophet has been and is accorded great respect and appreciation, pronouncements issuing from Joseph Smith have not been accepted automatically without critical appraisal. Thus Joseph Smith III, in writing of his father and other early leaders, wrote: "Our relation to these men as being their immediate successors demands of us, not a blind adherence to their views...but a full recognition of all their good thoughts, words, and acts... and acknowledgement of their errors, with a view to shun them."[5]

This right to reserve judgment extends to the church as a whole. Although Joseph Jr. had described baptism for the dead as "the most glorious of all subjects belonging to the everlasting gospel" (Doctrine and Covenants 110:17a, since removed by Conference action) the Reorganization treated the matter with considerable reservation and without commitment (see GCR 308, approved in 1886).

Those who ought to know say so (the appeal to reputation). Sometimes members will accord great deference to people who have been influential in their lives. Although this is understandable and fitting, it does not automatically invest those people with special authority. Nevertheless, individuals might say: "If Brother...says so, then it must be right." On occasion some persons might even claim themselves to be unimpeachable authorities. However, in general, members of the RLDS Church have been hesitant to grant authority in matters of belief merely on the basis of priesthood office or official position, or even of personal example. Such individuals might be respected, but our disposition has been to require beliefs to stand on their own feet and commend themselves. Certainly individuals are discouraged from appealing to their own office or position as grounds for validating their opinions.

It's been proved by experience (the appeal to experience). Observation of firsthand experience, or the reports of others is a valid source for theology. However, it is important to keep in mind, once again, that experience may be misread. It is common to hear the assertion that "seeing is believing." While there is substance to this point of view, it is also true that what is observed may be seriously impacted by prejudice, so it would be true to say that "believing is seeing." As previously noted, a person's established views, opinions, and experience might profoundly affect how an event is perceived. In fact, it is difficult to see how it could be otherwise. For many years I had understood from Doctrine and Covenants 42:12 that those who had faith to be healed were the ones who should request administration to the sick. This was the way my prejudiced view shaped my perception, even determining what I would see in print. I had to discipline my prejudice before I could understand that, in fact, it was those without faith to be healed who were advised to call for the elders.

Again, experience may be valid and dependable as far as it goes, but too narrow to allow proper conclusions to be drawn. One of our most common sources of error in thinking, not least of all theological thinking, is to reach conclusions using inadequate or even improper evidence. An individual might observe a single instance in which a male has appeared to exhibit greater wisdom than a female (if this is to be believed), and from this isolated instance draw a general conclusion that has no necessary basis in fact. It is not so long since people, with perfect seriousness, reached the conclusion that long hair among young males was proof of instability or immaturity. Experience can be a mixed blessing, especially if experience improperly interpreted or too narrowly founded leaves an individual with the illusion of having reached mature views "based on experience."

The most responsible thought follows when individuals draw upon a range of sources, are aware of what they are doing, and are conscious of the strengths and/or weaknesses attending each. Invariably the limitations will exist in the individual—lack of experience, ignorance of the scriptures, unfamiliarity with the tradition and decisions of the church, superficiality or prejudice in reasoning, timidity of faith. The sources are treasures to be mined and richly reward those who invest time and discipline in the effort.

---

3. Discuss and evaluate any or all of the sources for theological inquiry listed above, in terms of the strengths and weakness of each. It will be evident that the weaknesses are not in the sources themselves, but essentially in the application of them. Are there other sources that you have found helpful?

---

4. Can you cite examples, either in your own thinking or in that of others, when conclusions appear to have been drawn either from inadequate sampling or from prejudicial observation? How can you take precautions against drawing "tainted" conclusions?

Through a Glass Darkly

It is tempting and appealing to think that any one of us is capable of totally free and uncontaminated wisdom and insight. Such a person, whose confidence is only exceeded by naïveté, might say: "There's not a prejudiced bone in my body. I have come to my beliefs without any distorting influences. The Holy Spirit alone has been my guide." Genuine dialogue with such a person is extremely difficult, because positions are taken so firmly and irretrievably at the outset.

The truth of the matter is vastly different. Each of us exists as a particular (unique) individual in time and space. We inhabit a certain part of the earth in a certain period of time. We are creatures of history and culture, our social and intellectual formation predominantly shaped by the surrounding environment. Such an environment extends from our most immediate family and surroundings to the broadest reaches of our awareness of the world around us. A sixty-eight-year-old white Australian male member of the RLDS Church in the twentieth century does not experience the same world as a twenty-year-old African-American bondwoman of the nineteenth century who finds meaning in her Pentecostal Baptist congregation. Each of these individuals, and every other human being who occupies time and space in history, will view "reality" through a series of lenses, as it were. The lenses most likely will both illuminate and distort our perceptions of the world. It is stretching credulity to believe there is "one true perception," freed from all distortions of time, gender, class, tribe, religion, age, upbringing, or education. We will recognize the irony in the judgment of the white European traveler who, upon observing the inhabitants of a small island in the Pacific, wrote: "The natives of this island eat the strangest food, and their habits are disgusting." Nevertheless, while we may convey our prejudices in more sophisticated ways, even with the superficial trappings of education or experience, most of us are not too far removed from those people at whom we might be inclined to laugh.

It does not seem possible that we can be totally divorced from the particular body in which we are born, to become "citizens of the world." Nor can we translate ourselves into another time of history, despite the intriguing themes occasionally adapted for television or movies. It is difficult indeed for a Roman Catholic to "think" as a Latter Day Saint, and presumably the same holds true in reverse. Should one such person be converted to the faith of the other, vestiges of the original faith will linger, just as vestiges of my Australian heritage persist in me and will prevent me from ever fully experiencing the life of an American "from within." Perhaps the most that can be expected of any one of us is that we endeavor to be aware of and sensitive to the vastly different ways people inhabit their worlds.

---

5. Members of the class may wish to consider their own particularity in time and space, and venture to share with others how this might limit their perception of the world. Which areas of prejudice do you find it most difficult to conquer?

What does the foregoing have to say about the theological process? In the first place it should suggest that a certain modesty about the "almightiness" of one's own perceptions is in order. We will be hesitant to be too dogmatic or superior about the "strange" beliefs of our neighbors, or too supremely confident about own ability to be ultimately wise in our own convictions.

In the second place, the theological process will be enhanced immeasurably as people become willing to listen to each other, freed from the need for self-justification and defensiveness. Some years ago Harvey Cox suggested that the theologian might be helped by encountering a "rival sibling," somebody who represented a different worldview and was willing to enter into dialogue about the differences. Otherwise, religious groups (such as the RLDS) would tend to keep telling each other the things they like to hear each other say, because they have become so familiar to each other. The value of the "rival sibling" has been proved in settings where those from outside the RLDS tradition have been invited to serve as resource people at conferences and seminars. These participants invariably have been able to present a sympathetic yet honest view from another perspective, and to help us see ourselves as others see us. The inevitable outcome has been both a greater knowledge of and respect for each other. As church members have come face to face with alternative ways of asking the significant questions, or have been pressed to clarify their traditional meanings, new perspectives have surfaced. This has been described as the process of "picking up the stick by the other end."

The elders of the early Restoration church labored under the injunction that they were "not sent forth to be taught, but to teach" (Doctrine and Covenants 43:4b). This invariably was interpreted to mean that nobody could enlighten the members of the church on any conceivable matter of religious significance (although Joseph Smith himself did not hesitate to enlist the aid of resource people in the School of the Prophets). This stance, by no means unique to members of the Restoration movement, must have been seen by others as insufferable arrogance. Furthermore, there is no question that such a position closed off many opportunities for insight and learning.

The church undoubtedly has benefited from the participation of members, both men and women, at seminaries for advanced theological studies. Such institutions without known exception have respected the religious commitments of RLDS students and have made their resources available to provide the best possible experience for those students to serve in their chosen denominations. Our experience suggests that the most effective educational preparation for those wishing to serve the church professionally has been a combination of studies from both internal and external sources.

In the final analysis, at any point in time each person's beliefs will be the product of sources quite peculiar to that individual, coming together and forming a constellation of influences that the individual might or might not be able to explain completely. It is most likely that what a person comes to accept as authoritative is not determined by calculating the sum of the sources we have depended on. What is likely to be authoritative will be the way in which we sense a claim on our loyalty and commitment. The power and persuasiveness of that claim will exceed our ability to reduce it to language, yet it will be no less real for us. The preeminent English theologian and churchman John Baillie, in his posthumously published Gifford Lectures for 1961–1962, claimed that even more basic than our capacity to articulate beliefs is our sense of being claimed by a reality that, we are persuaded, exceeds every other reality:

> While indeed it seems impossible to enunciate any theoretical propositions concerning God and the unseen world about which we could be certain that they were true just as we enunciated them, nevertheless all our experience is "transfused with certitude"... [d]irect knowledge...is not knowledge of truths but knowledge of realities, and it is out of our immediate contact with these realities that certitude is born.[6]

Activities for the Reader

A. List in order of their importance for you the sources that have contributed to your present belief system. Indicate those you are currently making use of. Then mark which of these sources you would like to use more extensively. If possible, make a brief comment on each, suggesting what you can do to fulfill your wishes, given your present situation and opportunities. Your notes may include a wide range of resources: scripture study, Temple School courses, a personal journal, a study group, a friend with whom to share your search, a study of the book *Rules and Resolutions*, or one of the recently produced histories of the church: Richard Howard's *The Church Through the Years* (1992, 1993) or Paul Edwards's *Our Legacy of Faith* (1991). Be as honest as possible in evaluating your sources and as realistic as possible in outlining some plans for continuing your growth.

B. Construct a diagram that allows you to enumerate the several "lenses" through which you view the world. Then specify for each one (for example, your nationality, age, or gender) how this particular lense contributes positively to your view of reality, and also how it may hinder or diminish your capacity to understand. Which of the lenses do you consider most and least helpful?

Notes

1. Donald Walhout, *Interpreting Religion* (Englewood Cliffs, New Jersey: Prentice Hall, 1963), 43.
2. Arthur Oakman, "The Spirit of a Sound Mind," *Saints' Herald* 114, no. 16 (August 15, 1967):12.
3. Doctrine and Covenants 9:3a–c.
4. It was this interpretation of history that Roy Cheville challenged in his book *Did the Light Go Out?* (Independence, Missouri: Herald House, 1962).
5. *The True Latter Day Saints' Herald* 18, no. 23 (December 1, 1871): 723
6. John Baillie, *The Sense of the Presence of God* (London: Oxford University Press, 1962), 258.

Scripture Preview

A familiarity with scripture is a major resource for theology. This applies not only to the text of the scripture, but also to the background and development of the text as it has come to us. Indicate whether you believe each of the following statements to be true or false. The answers will be found on p. 202.

1. The Synoptic Gospels of the New Testament are Luke and John.   T   F
2. The Authorized Version of the Book of Mormon was published in 1966.   T   F
3. The RLDS Church is in possession of the original manuscript of the Book of Mormon.   T   F
4. The foreword to the Book of Mormon states that one of the purposes of the book is "to the convincing of the Jew and Gentile that Jesus is the Christ, the Son of the Eternal God."   T   F
5. The Authorized Version of the Book of Mormon published today by the RLDS Church is an exact reproduction (except for versification and punctuation) of the text as it was recorded by Joseph Smith Jr.   T   F
6. There are approximately 300 verses added to the Inspired Version that do not appear in the King James (Authorized) Version of the Bible, or that appear with changed wording.   T   F
7. The Book of Enoch, of interest to members of the early Restoration, and quoted in the New Testament (Jude 1:4) is available for study today.   T   F
8. The term "exegesis" means the critical examination and analysis of scriptural passages.   T   F
9. The term "higher criticism" describes the process of determining the most accurate form of the scriptural text, based on the examination of available manuscripts.   T   F

10. The RLDS Church has taken action to approve the Bible, the Book of Mormon, and the Doctrine and Covenants as the standard of authority on matters of church government and doctrine.   T   F

Chapter 6

According to the Scriptures

"You study the scriptures diligently, supposing that in having them you have eternal life; yet, although their testimony points to me, you refuse to come to me for that life."
—John 5:39–40, NEB

"Why aren't preachers and teachers content to say exactly what is in the scriptures, instead of adding their own interpretation? The scriptures are the word of God and shouldn't be interfered with."

—A listener in the pew

Very few writers ever committed themselves to paper (or its equivalent) with the expectation that what they wrote would eventually be accorded the status of "scripture." They might have written differently had they known. Instead they recorded stories, maintained court records, preserved genealogies, commented on current events, composed songs, wrote letters, and confessed their weaknesses (and those of others) with amazing candor. But above all they shared their testimonies of a transcendent power manifest in their personal and corporate history. Occasionally they sent messages in coded language to fellow believers. Without exception they might have been astonished to know that their writings would someday receive official endorsement and centuries later exercise a commanding authority in matters of belief and action, as well as stirring countless controversies, even to the shedding of blood.

The canonization of selected writings occurred for a variety of reasons. As it became increasingly apparent that the early Christian church was here to stay, it was considered necessary to provide authoritative sources to combat heresy and establish common belief and practice. Converts needed teaching in the faith, and future generations needed a source of reference. Over a period of centuries, and not without debate over certain books, the canon was established. With some variations it has retained the form specified by Athanasius in his Easter letter of A.D. 367.

Of course, the closing of the New Testament canon did not carry the implication that inspired writings had ceased, although biblical literalists have made this claim over the centuries. Their contention was that the canonical writings were somehow qualitatively different from other writings, inerrant and standing in a category by themselves. Without denying a particular and unique role to the canon, the English theologian Alan Richardson wrote many years ago:

> The inspiration of the Holy Spirit, in the sense in which St. Paul claimed to possess the Spirit's guidance, did not cease when the New Testament books were all written, or when the canon of the New Testament was finally drawn up; there is a wide range of Christian literature from the second to the twentieth century which can with propriety be described as inspired by the Holy Spirit in precisely the same formal sense as were the books of the Bible.[1]

---

1. Discuss the view expressed by Richardson. Traditionally Latter Day Saints have taken the view that inspiration ceased with the coming of the "apostasy" and was not experienced again until the time of the Restoration. Do you feel that this view can be sustained? Give reasons to support your point of view.

---

2. In your opinion are there noncanonical writings that, as Richardson says, could be termed "inspired"? If so, do you have specific choices that could be considered part of your personal "canon"? Why couldn't all inspired writings be collected under one cover?

Liberty of Conscience

Although there is no indication that an authoritative selection of Joseph Smith's messages to individuals and groups of church members was intended from the very beginning of the movement, the need for such a collection soon became evident. The original attempt to prepare such a collection was thwarted by the destruction of the printing press in Independence in July 1833. However, with some editing from the original text, an assembly of quorums approved an enlarged collection on August 7, 1835. This selection, along with the Book of Mormon and the "New Translation" of the Bible, was acknowledged in 1878 as "the standard of authority on all matters of church government and doctrine, and the final standard of reference on appeal in all controversies arising, or which may arise in this Church of Christ."[2]

Of course, members quickly discovered, as had other Christians over the centuries, that attributing authority to the scriptures could not end disputes or guarantee unanimity. Almost immediately it was necessary in subsequent General Conference resolutions to describe in more detail how the authority of scripture was to be understood and applied. The church affirmed the principle of "liberty of conscience" in recognizing the existence of differing points of view among the elders. At the same time preaching and teaching was to be limited, as far as possible, to the essentials:

> The elders should confine their teaching to such doctrines and tenets, church articles and practices, a knowledge of which is necessary to

obedience and salvation; and that in all questions upon which there is much controversy, and upon which the church has not clearly declared, and which are not unmistakably essential to salvation, the elders should refrain from teaching.[3]

Although, as previously noted, there was and has been no systematic attempt to specify just what these essentials might be, the scriptures have assumed a significant place in the life of the church, both in its missionary outreach and its congregational worship.

Interpretation: A Fact of Life

"The scriptures say..." is certainly one of the most commonly heard statements in religious discussion or debate. It is readily apparent that scripture is a basic reference and authority for the expression of belief. What is equally apparent, however, is that the meaning of scripture is rarely, if ever, self-evident or transparent in such a way that all people naturally derive the same meanings from the same passage.

This is to acknowledge the necessary and inevitable factor of *interpretation*. When anyone prefaces a statement by claiming, "The scriptures say," what should be added, at least mentally, is, "in my judgment, according to my background and study, as I have been influenced by parents and friends, by my religious affiliation, and by factors of which I may not even be aware."

Interpretation is a fact of life that must be lived with. It has been referred to previously as the pervading factor underlying all theological discussion and indeed virtually any kind of discussion. Occasionally this is obvious, because certain statements clearly defy simple explanation. Statements such as: "The children of this world are wiser in their generation, than the children of light" (Luke 16:8) or, "There is none good but one, that is, God" (Matthew 19:17) obviously call for scrutiny and interpretation. Paul's claim that "the earnest expectation of the creature waiteth for the manifestation of the sons of God"

(Romans 8:19) would certainly appear to justify Peter's observation that the apostle wrote some things "hard to be understood" (II Peter 3:16). Nevertheless, such apparently simple statements as: "God is love," "The just shall live by faith," or "Be ye perfect," lend themselves just as readily to varying interpretations. The person who accused the preacher of imposing her interpretation rather than keeping to the exact meaning of the scripture was asking for the impossible.

Interpretation is by no means a modern invention. As soon as people began to attach authority to certain writings, interpretation was necessary. Various methods or principles of interpretation have been advocated through the centuries. For example, Paul employed typology or allegory to link the Old Testament to the risen Christ. Jesus was the "second Adam," the church was the "new Israel," and the disciples were "the seed of Abraham." Robert M. Grant and David Tracy's book, *A Short History of the Interpretation of the Bible*,[4] provides a description of the predominant methods of interpretation (**hermeneutics**) employed through the centuries.

Over succeeding centuries scholars argued about the true nature of interpretation, or **exegesis**.[5] Origen claimed both a bodily and a spiritual sense for all scripture, with the latter concealed below the surface. Others denied any hidden meanings and affirmed the historical literalness of the record. In more recent times, "biblical criticism" has led to the identification of other criteria to be used in interpretation. Although the term "criticism" tended to convey a wrong impression, and although early biblical critics often exhibited an excess of zeal, the basic principles play an important part in discerning the meaning and significance of scripture. The actual text of the scripture is, of course, primary. Further, while the scripture is intended for analysis, it is essentially a witness: should the analysis suppress the witness, then the purpose of scripture has been subverted. However, it is important for serious students to understand the background against which the writings were produced, in order to avoid fundamental errors in interpretation.

Plenary Inspiration

Members of the Reorganization themselves pondered, and sometimes debated, the nature of the scriptural text. Joseph Smith shared little direct or detailed information regarding the process of producing the Book of Mormon or the reception of the inspired messages collected in the Doctrine and Covenants. Although the preface to the first edition of the New Translation claimed that the "translation and correction" were done "by direct revelation from God," it was not clear what conclusions could be drawn concerning the exact nature of the work, because notable revisions had been undertaken by Joseph Smith himself between the time of the first rendering of the several manuscripts and his death in 1844.[6] Recent scholarship has prompted writers to suggest caution in assuming that all revisions in the New Translation are "restorations" of some original text.[7]

The early debate, not unlike that under way in the wider Christian world in North America, centered on the question of **plenary** or **verbal** inspiration. Was the text of scripture to be understood as the directly communicated *words* of God, and thus by definition ultimate and inerrant? At the 1886 General Conference the following was approved as part of GCR 309: "That 'plenary inspiration' has never been affirmed by the church; but we believe in the so-named 'authorized' books of the church as a true and proper standard of evidence in the determination of all controverted doctrines in theology."

Church leaders, while respecting the scripture and according it significant authority, did not wish to be pressed into the obligation to regard the text as bearing the perfection and finality reserved for God alone. This view was underscored by Joseph Smith III when he gave evidence at the Temple Lot Suit in 1893, just seven years later. Regarding the New Translation he stated: "We do not consider it infallible, nor do we consider the Bible infallible. We do not consider anything that passes through human hands infallible. We do not believe in the plenary inspiration of the Bible."[8]

In more recent years also, examination of the manuscript data related to the Three Standard Books has helped us perceive more accurately the process behind the actual printed word. Richard Howard's detailed study of the manuscript materials—as well as careful exploration of the nature of revelation, inspiration, and scripture by such church leaders as F. Henry Edwards, Roy Cheville, Arthur Oakman, Duane Couey, Walter Johnson, and a younger generation of professionally trained scholars—provides a strong resource for us as members of the Reorganized Church in our approach to scriptural interpretation.

---

3. Do you depend on any resource materials (dictionaries, concordances, commentaries) in your study of the scriptures? Share these with other members of the class.

4. Why do you think church members tended to insist on a literal view of scripture, despite the long tradition embedded in Conference resolutions and other statements cautioning against this view? Has the recent resurgence of fundamental Christianity, generally affirming the inerrancy of scripture, had any influence on members of your congregation?

Guidelines for Interpretation

Responsible guidelines for interpretation are necessary. The "Word of God" has too often been invoked to support or justify interpretations that have become an embarrassment or an offense. Individuals and institutions have justified slavery, white supremacy, "justifiable" homicide, male superiority, celibacy, "one true church," and the withholding of life-giving drugs or blood transfusions all in the name of scripture. Questionable interpretations of prophecies (from which Reorganized Church members have not been free) have raised their confusions and left their disillusionments.

Scriptural interpretation is rarely a matter for interesting conversation or casual dialogue. People are generally deeply invested in their positions. The process can be intense, and differences become heated, sometimes malicious, and occasionally deadly. The following guidelines, expressed as a series of questions, may prove helpful in the search for honest and responsible interpretation.

What is the most accurate form of the text?

This task, sometimes called "lower criticism," concerns the actual form of the text. This may be most important with the Bible which has a long and complex history. Where did the Gospel of Mark originally end? What verses appear to have come on the scene after the first manuscripts? At the same time, it will be important to recognize that textual variations have occurred in the Book of Mormon, Doctrine and Covenants, and New Translation through various editions. Did Joseph Smith intend, for example, for the text of II Nephi 12:84 to read "white and delightsome" or "pure and delightsome?" It appears that the committee producing the 1908 edition overrode Joseph's wishes and chose the first wording. What textual variations occurred in Sections 3, 5, 8, 17, and 42 of the Doctrine and Covenants, and why did the name of Frederick G. Williams replace Jesse Gauze as a member of the First Presidency in 1832 (Section 80, March 1832)?

What is the setting for the text?

"Higher criticism" deals with questions of authorship, date, intended audience, circumstances of writing, cultural setting, and historical background. Scripture arises not in a vacuum but against the background of and often in specific response to particular events, issues, and situations. Who were the "grievous wolves" vilified by Paul in Acts 20:29? What did it mean to "heap coals of fire upon the head" as being the result of an act of kindness (Romans 12:20)? Who was the author of Hebrews? How many authors contributed to the book of Isaiah as it presently appears? Why did the earliest manuscripts of Mark end at verse 8 of chapter 16? Scripture commentaries and dictionaries will invariably provide important data for the interpreter.

Does the text have universal or particular application?

Is the passage to be applied directly to and authoritative for all times and circumstances, or should it be understood in reference to a particular cultural or historical situation? Is the prohibition of certain musical instruments during prayer meetings universal, or might it be eventually removed, as F. Henry Edwards suggested some years ago?[9] Is Paul's teaching regarding the superiority of celibacy (I Corinthians 7) still universal and valid? Should women who pray or prophesy with their heads uncovered still be shorn (I Corinthians 11:5–6)? How universal is the commandment in Doctrine and Covenants 42:12a that garments should be plain and homemade? Does the advice in Doctrine and Covenants 147:7 regarding the evaluation and further reinterpretation of principles apply universally, or specifically to World Conference representation?

What prejudices (prior assumptions) do I bring to the interpretation?

No one is free of prejudice—judgments already shaped by previous experience. Strictly speaking, we each approach scripture not with an "open mind" but with one that is a storehouse of accumulated ideas, attitudes, convictions, values, and needs. Such prejudgments will hinder interpretation unless we are at least aware of their existence and make an honest attempt to allow for them. Striving to give earnest consideration to points of view from those whose background, experience, and allegiances differ from our own is crucial, because the great bulk of scripture was written by just such people.

5. Discuss the contribution of higher and lower criticism toward more accurate interpretation of the scriptures. How do these disciplines apply to the Inspired Version, Book of Mormon, and Doctrine and Covenants? Share with others what you know about specific instances.

6. Consider the examples given on the need to determine whether specific passages of scripture are universal or limited in their application. Mention other examples that you think may be limited to a specific time rather than universal. Why is it important to make the effort to distinguish between the universal (binding for all times, everywhere) or limited to particular circumstances?

What are my emotional investments in specific interpretations?

Do I find myself becoming irritated, angry, or threatened when cherished notions are confronted? Do I impute ignorance or evil to those who differ? Do I assume that my motives, as contrasted with others, are pure, and that mine is the one true interpretation?

Am I alert to new or previously unnoticed nuances in the text?

Have I noted, for example, that the oft-quoted passage prohibiting women from speaking or ruling is followed by the generally ignored phrase, "as also saith the law"? Have I considered why Paul should quote Jewish law in addressing Christian congregations? Have I carefully read the passage (in Doctrine and Covenants 42:12c, d) that specifies it is those who "have *not* faith to be healed, but believe" who are to receive administration by the elders of the church? Very often it is the part of the passage that is *not* attended to that needs special attention.

Do I consult differing versions for clarification?

Archaic language and difficult constructions may often be clarified by a modern English or popular version. At times the very freshness and unfamiliarity of the wording will illuminate meanings that have been obscured by familiarity with the traditional text. So, for instance, reference to a modern English version would clarify the meaning of Romans 8:19, just as it would help us understand the different sense in which the word "prevent" is used in I Thessalonians 4:15.

How much does it matter?

Does the text demand a final answer? Is it a matter of burning importance? Is it important enough that I will risk jeopardizing valued relationships to establish the supremacy of my interpretation? When dealing with the question of the resurrection, as noted in the last chapter, the Conference supported the view that it was *"of doubtful propriety for the church to put unnecessary restrictions upon the ministry as to the manner of their teaching those doctrines and matters of faith which are of secondary importance."* As a youth growing up in the church, I recall heated and sometimes acrimonious debates on such matters as soul-sleeping, the Sabbath, and the interpretations of prophecies—issues that raised blood pressure but did little to strengthen the saint or convert the sinner.

What is the authority of this passage for my life?

This is perhaps the most important factor of all. What effect does it have on the way I conduct my life? What would it mean for me to take the passage with the utmost seriousness? Am I committed to this particular passage because I want to change somebody else's opinion, or because I want to deepen my understanding, perhaps even change my life? It is not uncommon for the texts that yield readily to understanding (interpretation) to be most readily ignored, as, for example, Matthew 18:22.

---

7. Discuss the use of different versions of the Bible, identifying particular values associated with each. Would it be helpful to have different versions of the Book of Mormon or Doctrine and Covenants? In what ways might the versions differ?
8. The text suggests that the most important question may be the bearing that scripture has on the conduct of one's life. Can you identify particular parts of the scripture that contain challenges that you find difficult to implement, even though you are convinced they are true? How do you deal with such situations?

The Ongoing Quest

The task of responsible interpretation requires a high degree of competence and commitment. While respecting the scriptures, church leaders have declined to identify an absolute authority, infallible in matters of interpretation. We attribute authority to the Holy Spirit but acknowledge that the Spirit does not seem to pronounce the truth in ways that are equally and universally accepted by all members.

One final observation may be appropriate. In affirming and practicing an open canon of scripture, members of the church will on occasion experience a tension between the traditional and familiar on the one hand and the new and unexpected on the other. F. Henry Edwards expressed this insight some time ago in a discussion of scripture and revelation:

It is much easier to try to live by past revelation, which is hoary with the weight of years and contained forever in a book, than it is to live for constantly fresh and challenging revelations which take note of the expanding means of understanding which the years have brought, and require us to march purposefully toward new high lands of understanding.[10]

People committed to responsible scriptural understanding will experience both the pain and promise of that tension.

Activities for the Reader

A. Select a book from the Bible, a section from the Doctrine and Covenants, or a book from the Book of Mormon. Apply, using whatever resources you can secure, the disciplines of higher criticism to the material, making notes of your findings. When you have finished, make a brief notation stating how the process has enhanced your appreciation of the scripture chosen. Also note any questions that may have arisen as a result of your study.

B. Volunteer to lead a ten-minute discussion on a section of the chapter in class. Make an outline of your presentation in your notebook.

Notes

1. Alan Richardson, *Christian Apologetics* (Philadelphia: SCM Press, 1947), 207.
2. General Conference Resolution 215 (September 13, 1878).
3. General Conference Resolution 222 (September 29, 1879).
4. Robert M. Grant and David Tracy, *A Short History of the Interpretation of the Bible* (Minneapolis, Minnesota: Augsburg Fortress, 1984). It is noteworthy that this brief survey describes fourteen systems of interpretation employed over this period of time.
5. Strictly speaking, "hermeneutics" denotes the general system of interpretation employed, while "exegesis" refers to the analysis of the meaning of given passages, using a specific system.
6. Richard P. Howard's masterful study, *Restoration Scriptures: A Study of Their Textual Development*, Second Edition, Revised and Enlarged (Independence, Missouri: Herald House, 1995), when first published in 1969, introduced a ma-

jor new dimension to the study and understanding of the church's scriptures and a related doctrine of revelation.

7. F. Henry Edwards, "The Inspired Version Today," *Saints' Herald* 114, no. 24 (December 15, 1967):15–17; Richard B. Lancaster, James E. Lancaster, and Donald D. Landon in *The Old Testament Speaks to Our Day* (Senior High Teacher's Manual, 1960), 27–28; Robert J. Matthews, *"A Plainer Translation": Joseph Smith's Translation of the Bible, A History and Commentary* (Provo, Utah: Brigham Young University Press, 1975), 253.

8. Abstract of Evidence, Section 158: 493.

9. F. Henry Edwards, *A New Commentary on the Doctrine and Covenants* (Independence, Missouri: Herald House, 1977), 425–426.

10. F. Henry Edwards, *A Commentary on the Doctrine and Covenants* (Independence, Missouri: Herald House, 1958), 10.

Chapter 7

Theology in the RLDS Community

"Once a matter has been discussed at Conference and the majority vote has established the truth of the matter, I don't see why the minority just shouldn't accept it so the church can move forward in a unified manner. People who still can't accept what has been decided are just lacking in faith."

—Overheard at World Conference

"There is no absolute tribunal this side of the great judgment day that is authorized to determine exactly who is right and who is wrong in a dispute or controversy, such as arises frequently in our midst."

—Joseph Smith III (1910)

In the realm of the exchange of opinions on matters of belief and practice the Reorganization has established some critical principles that have to do both with individual freedom and with personal responsibility. In a community such as the Reorganized Church, a balance between these two life dimensions is profoundly important. Their observance will open the way to a richer community; their neglect or negation will result in disruption and heartache in the body.

Although there is considerable dialogue from time to time between Christians of different faiths or between Christians and practioners of other world religions, theology for most of us is carried on in the context of a faith community. We do not deal with a generic brand of faith but with that expression of truth that is most immediately discerned in our own fellowship. It is this fellowship that provides, for most of us and for most of the time, the framework, the common story, the common experience, and the unique faith symbols that nurture us. We do not discuss truth *in general*, though we would like to believe that the truth we discern is generally appropriate, and consistent with the best insights emerging from other communities.

This is the perspective that Daniel Migliori has pointed out emphatically in the preface to his book on the theological enterprise:

> The point is that theological inquiry does not arise in a vacuum. It is not built on amorphous religious experiences or on the pious imaginations of isolated individuals. On the contrary, the work of theology is inseparably bound to an identifiable faith community that worships God, attends to Scripture and its accounts of God's work and will, and engages in manifold ministries of education, reconciliation, and liberation. In short, theological inquiry requires continuing participation in the common life of a community of faith, prayer, and service. Apart from such participation, theology would soon become an empty exercise.[1]

What, then, are the particular parameters of theological discourse in the Reorganized Church? What are the rules and guidelines for "playing fair"? And how are they intended to facilitate the most fruitful interchange in the search for truth and nurture the relationship between those engaged in the search?

Freedom of Conscience

The freedom of the individual member to his or her belief without coercion, harassment, or judgment from others is a principle that has been virtually coterminous with the life of the Reorganization. It is hinted at in the statement by Joseph

Smith III in the introduction to this chapter, made after a half-century of leading the church. That the matter had long been on the prophet's mind is reflected in the fact that this statement, made to the General Conference of 1910, is remarkably similar to that made many years previously during the Temple Lot Suit. He went on to say:

> Hence it devolves upon us to carry our differences without animosity, without fault-finding, without charging evil intent or purpose upon those who may differ from us. I have tried to impress this thought upon you and upon others, and I want now to have you think upon it....
>
> There is no tribunal—I want you to remember this affirmation and I hope those representatives of the press will quote me as I state it now—there is no tribunal, this side of the great judgment bar, that has the authorized right to sit in judgment upon the faith of men and say whether or not they are heterodox or orthodox....
>
> This makes every man responsible to God. He has a secondary responsibility to those with whom he is associated...in labor or work, to observe their rights, while assuming those which he deemed to belong to himself.[2]

Several features of this statement are worth noting. First, the emphatic tone of the president's speech. Second, his concern to be quoted correctly by reporters attending the conference. Third, the fact that the president admits to having made this appeal previously, implying that the advice had not been accepted as readily as he had hoped. In the fourth place, President Smith made it clear that a person's primary responsibility was to God, and only secondarily to fellow members. And finally, the foundation upon which all the other elements rested: the need to have mutual respect for personal rights. It is also worth noting that in the face of occasional charges that in the "old days" peace and harmony reigned among the Saints, Joseph frankly acknowledged that even in those far-off times disputes and controversies arose "frequently." Dissent is no new arrival on the scene of church life. If anything, we have gradu-

ally learned how to handle debate or dispute with increased
sensitivity.

> 1. Review the statement made by Joseph Smith III at
>   the 1910 Conference. What were the points of con-
>   cern he identified? Do you consider his words may
>   have been directed primarily to members regarding
>   their relations toward each other in the church, or in
>   their relations to others outside the Reorganization,
>   or to both? What would have occasioned his re-
>   peated treatment of this theme? Would you say his
>   advice generally has been heeded through the years?

The principle of freedom of conscience has been upheld frequently, in Conference enactments, church literature, and in the
Doctrine and Covenants. It is a privilege that most members
would claim for themselves but that many seem reluctant to
extend to others. When a member wrote to the First Presidency
(*Saints' Herald* 37, p. 97), deploring the difference of opinion
existing among some members, the prophet replied:

> If nothing were said or written until all the brethren and all men were
> of one opinion on a given topic, where and how would there ever be
> an interchange? If all differences of opinion are to be construed into
> contention, how shall unity be reached?... The elders have long been
> fighting the "one man idea," and contending for the sacredness of the
> personal right to think and act, and why should we now object to what
> must always be the result of individual thinking, diversity of idea and
> conclusion?... If [they] saw all things exactly alike, the argument
> would be almost irresistible that the field of vision was very limited,
> or the range restricted by personal inability to see much or see far.[3]

Joseph was not impressed by claims that the church in the
time of the founder had been free of dissent, and that there was
greater unanimity of opinion in the early years of the church,
before 1844. Although troubled by dissent when it seemed to
reach major proportions and sought a stronger centralized au-

thority (see chapter 11), he generally supported free and vigorous debate, convinced that this should be possible without animosity or divisiveness. He was skeptical of those who complained about disunity, and yet who themselves expressed opinions and judgments that were opposed to the views expressed by leaders. His question when this occurred was: "Who is the dissenter: those expressing their views or those expressing disagreement?" In a *Saints' Herald* editorial he observed:

> It is very curious that men can deplore differences of opinion and the expression of such difference, and yet be the first to dissent from the expressed opinion of others. Very curious indeed that such men and brethren should charge this difference as evidence of want of unity in love and good fellowship. To us, one of the most comprehensible evidences of good-fellowship that any people can show is the ability to abide in co-labor, conscious of each others opinions and tolerant of them.[4]

It is possible that Joseph Smith III was broader in his practice of tolerance than many of his contemporaries felt comfortable with. In an age of debate, within the church and against representatives of other faiths, Joseph repeatedly advised moderation and mutual regard. Both priesthood officers and members tended to be critical of their fellows who did not conform to expectations, and sought the president's support for their complaints. When a church member wrote to ask whether a person could be a true Latter Day Saint and yet have reservations about the Book of Mormon, New Translation of the Bible, and Doctrine and Covenants as inspired, he replied:

> A man fully imbued with the genius and spirit of the Latter Day Work, will undoubtedly have and receive a good degree of faith in the books referred to; but we think it quite possible for a man to be fully impressed with the truth of the Latter Day Work, that Jesus is the Christ, and the gospel true, and know very little about the Book of Mormon, or Doctrine and Covenants, or be undecided and doubtful about them. We know some just such, who are excellent men, who will make every sacrifice for the sake of the cause.[5]

It is abundantly clear that the right of personal conscience is deeply embedded in the tradition of the Reorganization. We have defended vigorously the freedom to express one's opinion, the freedom to differ, and even the freedom to be in error without condemnation. Such freedoms are vital not only to the legislative process and the making of decisions, but equally so in the dialogue on matters of faith and belief. Whether members have lived up to and prospered from the practice of these principles in the jurisdictions of the church must itself be a matter of opinion.

---

2. To what extent do you believe the freedoms mentioned above have been observed and consciously cultivated in the life of the church, both in the church at large and in the congregations? Do you feel that our discussion of potentially divisive issues is sometimes avoided because of fear of disunity?

Minorities Are Members, Too

A community such as the church, which accords great value to each member, must also preserve the value of minorities, whether in the legislative assemblies, or in the sharing of concepts in the theological process. It is a fact that even while "majorities" can be quite accepting and sensitive to the rights of minorities in voting matters, they may be less accepting and even condemning if ideas surface from a single member or if a small number of such "nonconforming" members are discerned in congregations. As regrettable as it might be, it is not unheard of for people to be excluded from the fellowship, albeit subtly, for views that engendered discomfort or disapproval in assemblies of the Saints.

It may be appealing to believe that majorities are necessarily right, either on a conference floor or in a church school class. A statement in the Book of Mormon appears to suggest that this is generally true:

> Now it is not common that the voice of the people desireth anything contrary to that which is right; but it is common for the lesser part of the people to desire that which is not right; Therefore this shall ye observe, and make it your law to do your business by the voice of the people.[6]

Most people would tend to agree, until perhaps they find themselves in the minority on a particular issue or debate, and then they see the rights of the minority in a different light. People tend to be so supremely confident of the rightness of their position that it is extremely difficult to support decisions made by a majority without disappointment, resentment, or criticism of those who have prevailed. This will hold especially true if decisions made by majorities are genuinely offensive to the conscience of those whose will is frustrated.

One might accept the general principle cited above, which reflects great confidence in the judgments of majorities. Nevertheless, not only may a minority be occasionally (or frequently) right, but there is no infallible authority who can make that determination, as Joseph Smith III asserted. A majority vote does not establish truth, correctness, or wisdom; it expresses a commitment to specific views or courses of action based on the judgment of the members.

In the same way, majorities are not, by definition, those who unerringly proclaim truth and light. It has been observed that new ideas are rarely applauded by large majorities of people, either in the realm of religion or in life generally. Often such ideas must enter the world under the burden of illegitimacy, and must persist and persuade on the way to respectability. This is the reality borne out repeatedly in the course of history. Even the concept of religious freedom, accepted as one of the cornerstones of a democratic society, did not immediately win support in the new American nation. One of the great virtues of common consent, and the right of all people to be heard, is that the process leaves the door open for ideas to be tested and vindicated. Time not only vindicates the prophet, it verifies ideas, concepts, and practices that enrich the human spirit. Tragically, when differences occur, divisions are often created in the heat of dissent without giving an idea its opportunity to move toward common consent. Once positions have been firmly taken, and harsh words of condemnation spoken, it is difficult to retract those accusations and allow healing to take place.

For this reason it is appropriate to suggest that the church is wise to embrace and protect its minorities, not in any condescending way, but as vital members of the community, who should be able to speak without duress and be listened to without resentment. Of course, an equal responsibility rests with those who may constitute the minority on any issue. It is well to keep in mind that given the way in which ideas often win acceptance (gradually), the difference in being part of a majority or a minority may essentially be a matter of timing. Minorities may be the vanguard of the church's growing edge.

---

3. Are there, from time to time, minorities, even minorities of one, in the RLDS communities with which you are familiar? Is there opportunity for their presence to be respected and their voice to be heard? What do they contribute to the life of the church?
4. In the British parliamentary system, the minority party functions as "a loyal opposition." How might this concept enhance the program of the church when controversial issues are considered and voted on?

Responsible Participation

If the principle of personal conscience is not balanced by the practice of responsible participation, freedom deteriorates into license, with inevitable injury to both people and ideas. Decisions written into the scripture and Conference enactments provide guidance in the delicate matter of balancing freedom and accountability.

In the first place, there are appropriate places and circumstances for people to exercise their right to free speech. Members are not free to take advantage of the public arenas of the church to carry debates from the legislative assembly into the congregations, in order to extol or advance their viewpoints. This holds whether the matter is payment of the Graceland debt, as in the following reference, or dealing with the name of the church or the ordination of women.

> The ministers going out from the conferences held by the elders of my church are not expected or authorized to throw obstacles in the way of the accomplishment of that which has been intrusted to the Bishopric to pay this great debt. Their right to free speech, their right to liberty of conscience, does not permit them as individuals to frustrate the commands of the body in conference assembly. They are sent out as ministers to preach the gospel, and their voices if opposed to what may be presented to the conference should be heard in the conferences, and not in the mission fields....[7]

Some years before this principle was reaffirmed by the approval of the 1901 Conference, a similar position had been advocated for the sharing of beliefs in the church's official publication. The Conference of 1885 made this determination:

> That in our opinion there is a just and proper line to be drawn between the position of permitting a fair hearing of the views of any and all through the church paper, and the abuse of the sacred principle of toleration and freedom adhered to by the church by using to excess the columns of the church paper, in making a series of attacks upon the life of the body, or an undue effort to enforce personal views upon the people, when they are clearly in part antagonistic to the accepted faith of the body.[8]

The very next year, the Conference again addressed the matter of freedom and the limitations of free speech. It was clear that members had no license to say whatever they might wish or choose to say, without regard for the welfare of the body. The following was adopted:

That the presentation of individual opinions by elders, or others of the body, such as opinions not having been affirmed by the body as a rule of faith or practice, does not make them a part of the faith or belief of the body; but relate to us individually upon the issue of toleration, which toleration, we believe as was manifested in the action of Jesus while dealing with men here in his ministry, should be so broad as to make no occasion for persons to wish to withdraw from the body by reason of these individual differences of opinion.[9]

Thus the principle of personal conscience must be upheld, but with respect for decisions properly arrived at, and for the rights of other people. This requirement was clearly affirmed by Joseph Smith III in the course of sharing his last revelatory document with the church:

Those who go out from the assemblies and solemn conclaves of the church should exercise great care in their ministration abroad both to the branches where they may officiate and in their preaching the gospel to those outside, to avoid sowing seeds of distrust and suspicion either in public ministration or in private conversation.[10]

Religious judgments and convictions are profoundly important to the people who hold them. When differences occur between those who are supposedly committed to the same cause there may be strong temptations to belittle ideas and demean people who are seen as responsible for the differences. Labels and charges of various kinds require little thought and can easily come to the lips. "What else would you expect from one of those fundamentalists (or liberals)!" "He only says that because...." "She's just one of those radical feminists." The dialogue is carried out at its highest level when participants are able to assume acceptance, trust, a willingness to listen, and an absence of innuendo or labels.

Equally important is the provision of settings for informal dialogue, so that people do not feel voiceless. Formal church services rarely provide this kind of setting, and issues may go unexamined. Members may wish to avoid the stress of confrontation, and so bypass dialogue in the congregations, preferring such discussion to be left to the larger assemblies of Saints and apart from fellow members and family they see every Sunday "up close and personal."

---

5. A concerned member asks: "But if I feel strongly about my viewpoint, why shouldn't I be permitted to speak up in public? I wasn't able to be at the conference, and shouldn't be penalized for that." Discuss this member's concern.

6. Another member asks: "If we are Christ's church, should we not expect the Holy Spirit to show us what is right, instead of having to endure this unseemly contention? After all, I hold the belief I do because the Holy Spirit has led me to see the truth, and it should be the same for everybody who trusts in God." Respond to this member's question.

A particular challenge attends members of the Reorganization, arising from its belief in an open canon. This belief has several implications. In the first place, revelatory documents coming to the church sometimes confront members with new ideas, or with new understandings of old ideas at relatively short notice. It is one thing to sing confidently: "The Lord hath yet more light and truth, to break forth...." It is another thing to be faced with the possibility that this might actually be happening, even though, as noted above, the "light and truth" may have been breaking forth for some time before it is widely recognized and accepted.

111

Again, although the church has declined to commit itself to the concept of plenary inspiration by GCR 308, the form of language in which communications are most frequently shared may reinforce a view of verbal inspiration in the minds of many members. Thus it is not unusual for one to say, when citing some reference from the Doctrine and Covenants: "But God has said...." This carries the imputation that anybody questioning or opposing such a reference is opposed to God, which is a heavy burden to bear. Not infrequently, presidents of the church bringing such documents to the Conference have been careful, in their prefatory remarks, to encourage a broader view of the revelatory process, but such advice can all too easily be ignored.

In this connection, one particular issue needs to be mentioned. Although members of the church may be prepared to question the prescriptive authority and infallible status of "ancient" scripture, they may not be inclined to consider "modern" scripture—i.e., the Doctrine and Covenants or revisions appearing in the New Translation—with the same reservations. It is one thing to be able to say, with the wisdom of hindsight: "Well, that's just the way they thought in those times." It is another thing to acknowledge the historical/cultural impact on our contemporary views, particularly if they carry the weight of scriptural approval. So members might not feel obligated to accept as binding the directive to stone disobedient children (Deuteronomy 21:18, 21) but might grant the status of infallibility to the provisions regarding stakes, or to women in the priesthood, or to the alternative rendition of the "second mile" reference in Matthew 5:43 IV, or to the Mosaic authorship of the Pentateuch.

A Standard or a Guide?

The traditional use of the term "standard books" to refer to the scriptural resources of the church has tended to impose an unduly prescriptive status on those resources, reinforced by the tendency to uphold the notion of plenary inspiration. It is sometimes difficult to hold respect for the scripture and the recognition of its humanness in balance. It was the tendency to attribute to scripture the status of absolute and final answers that prompted F. Henry Edwards to include the following in an early edition of his commentary on the Doctrine and Covenants:

> It is because our natural spiritual inertia has thus led us to seek a standard rather than a guide, that a theory of revelation has grown up which regards the Bible as the infallible and final revelation of the will of God. This theory is not true to experience, nor to the claims of the divine word itself.[11]

For members of the Reorganization, this same temptation holds with respect to those books that have been accepted as "standard." The temptation to desire a standard rather than a guide may be virtually irresistible. To hold to the best we can know at any point in time, while remaining open to the ongoing search for new truth, is a stance that requires faith and courage.

It may seem that this chapter has been unduly burdened with citations from our history and from Conference resolutions. The intent has been to identify principles and precedents that have been long established in our movement, though sometimes overlooked in the "heat of battle." Significant guidelines and decisions laid down in the first generations of the Reorganization have served us remarkably well when allowed to operate in the right spirit, especially in a pluralistic community such as the contemporary church has become.

Activities for the Reader

A. Review *Rules and Resolutions* to find those that relate to the freedoms and responsibilities of church members in the matter of church belief and doctrine. Make a brief list of the principles found in these resolutions.

B. Read Sections 125, 130, and 131 of the Doctrine and Covenants. Summarize the statements found in these resolutions describing the appropriate behavior of church members relating to decisions reached by the church. You may wish to gather in separate lists the "shoulds" and the "should nots." Are there additional guidelines, in either category, that you think could be added to these lists? If you are interested you can consult F. Henry Edwards's *Commentary on the Doctrine and Covenants* to find the background to these sections.

Notes

1. Daniel L. Migliori. *Faith Seeking Understanding: An Introduction to Christian Theology* (Grand Rapids, Michigan: Wm. B. Eerdmans, 1991), xii.
2. Joseph Smith III, *Saints' Herald* 57, no. 17 (April 27, 1910): 417–418.
3. *Saints' Herald* 37, no. 7 (February 15, 1890): 97.
4. Ibid., 29, no. 11 (June 1, 1882): 174.
5. Ibid., 24, no. 10 (May 15, 1877): 153.
6. Mosiah 13:35–36.
7. Doctrine and Covenants 125: 16a, b, c (1901).
8. General Conference Resolution 298:2 (adopted April 10, 1885).
9. General Conference Resolution 308:1 (adopted April 9, 1886).
10. Doctrine and Covenants 131:4b (1914).
11. F. Henry Edwards, *A Commentary on the Doctrine and Covenants* (Independence, Missouri: Herald House, 1958), 10.

Chapter 8

Disciplines for the Task

So often, in theological wars,
  The disputants, I ween,
Rail on in utter ignorance
  Of things each other mean,
And prate about an elephant
  No one has ever seen.

— G. S. Saxe, "The Blind Man
and the Elephant"

"Appoint among yourselves a teacher, and let not all be spokesmen at once, but let one speak at a time, and let all listen unto his sayings, that when all have spoken, that all may be edified of all, and that every man may have an equal privilege."

— Doctrine and Covenants 85:37b
(The "Olive Leaf" revelation)

While many people would admit that theology is a demanding discipline, they might wish to limit such labors to the professional student or theologian. For the rest of us it might be regarded simply as a matter of chatting about what's on our minds, or what has been scheduled as the class material for the day, without calling for any particular skills or disciplines. Theological exploration might almost be thought of as "doing what comes naturally," with little need for deliberate forethought or preparation. Indeed, many of us may have found theological reflection so difficult that it is better left alone. It is sufficient, we might persuade ourselves, to depend on what we learned at an earlier age, or when we first became members of the church.

Although I have referred to various theological disciplines at previous points in this study, in this chapter I will attempt to draw together those I consider most important. Each person might realize that they already possess some of these in the form of gifts, which nevertheless need to be cultivated. Other disciplines may require conscious effort to develop. Whatever the case, the church depends on the presence of a sufficient number of people in each congregation who are willing to commit time and effort to the task. "Behold, I stand at the door and knock" is clearly an invitation to participate in the theological venture.

Preserving the Tradition

The readiness to preserve a lively tradition is fundamental to the theological task. We must admit that "tradition" has not received great respect in recent times. However, tradition does not essentially involve maintaining dead ideas and forms of the past, as implied in the famous song from *Fiddler on the Roof*. Rather, it refers to the authority established in the past, which yet affects our unfinished future; it has to do with the prospect of "ignoring" what is considered to be most significant in the life of the community. In this sense, memory is the fulcrum of freedom, a lively ongoing dialogue with one's unique story. Meaning and identity are essentially bonded by story, rather than by theory. The power of narrative, embracing both our personal and corporate narratives, is that it enables us to be responsive to the illuminating dimensions of our past. These reveal what Anthony Chvala-Smith has called our "core values."[1]

In one sense it is true, as George Santayana observed, that "those who cannot remember the past are condemned to repeat it."[2] In the field of theology this may mean that individuals will persist in the promotion of ideas that experience has long since shown unable to stand the test of time. Latter Day Saints have suffered from their inclination to dismiss more than 1,500 years of church history as of no consequence, as if ideas and insights ground to a halt at the onset of the "apostasy." But even granting this, church members have been little acquainted with the preceding centuries, embracing a wide range of fruitful thought and writing extending as far back as the early Christian Fathers. This would explain why, for many RLDS students attending theological seminary (such as myself), the exposure to church history and thought has served as a giant "aha." Not least of the "revelations" such a study provides is the recognition that many others have endured the same struggles, encountered the same difficulties, and sometimes made the same errors we have made. To realize this is to feel less superior toward others on whom we might casually pass judgment; it is also to derive encouragement from the recognition that we have not been alone in the journey.

However, there is another dimension to our lively dialogue with the past. Not only might we be kept from preserving ideas that have failed to withstand the test of time. Equally important, we shall be opened to the richness of a past that can tell us where we have come from, who we now are, and where we want to go. In a *Christian Century* Pentecost meditation, the origin of which I have regretfully failed to locate, the following plea is made for the historical consciousness:

> The struggle of history is the struggle of memory to prevail over forgetfulness. The loss of history is the loss of memory; it is the triumph of the airbrush, the triumph of the void. We must protect our own histories from being airbrushed and voided. We need our memories in order to understand who we are.... One builds the relationship between memory and hope through retaining and creating a past that gives meaning and significance to the present.[3]

1. To what extent does your own personal family story, your unique personal history, help you to understand where you have come from, who you are, and where you wish to go? Are there stories or accounts of your past that hold special significance for your life journey? Members of the group may choose to share some of these.

2. To what extent have you personally, or the congregation(s) you have belonged to, entered into a "lively" dialogue about the story of the church? Has there been an openness to the exploration, including the reinterpretation of our history, or is it generally considered of little relevance except for defending the authority of the Restoration movement?

By Study and by Faith

The enhancement of learning by the processes of studying and "faithing" has been lifted up several times in this study. I have expressed the relationship in this particular way to emphasize the point of view that both are active processes. This should help defuse the notion that whereas study can be demanding and burdensome, faith is just a matter of "possessing" some quality that relieves us of the need to invest time and energy.

The disciplines related to study are obvious. They involve setting time aside for reading, meditating, and testing our apprehension of what we have read. They may well involve formal course work, such as offered by the Temple School Center or other institutions of learning, including theological seminaries. Discussion about mutually acceptable themes may be a significant aspect of learning, either in a mentor relationship or in other congregational settings. The accumulation of general references and books dealing with specific subjects will be important. In the midst of competing demands from busy schedules, the discipline of study will call for intentional commitments of time, if it is not to "fall through the cracks."

Our daughter, a Graceland nursing graduate working in the cardiac unit of a Kansas City hospital, must periodically undergo continuing education. The welfare of her patients is at stake. In the face of potential malpractice litigation, she must be well qualified and up-to-date before being let loose on the public, so to speak. The deed would seem no less critical for those who claim to order their lives responsibly and who relate to others with the testimony of living by a profound truth. In a world that expects and demands competence, practitioners of the faith should set a high priority on excellence in their explications of the gospel.

The discipline of "faithing" may well be equally demanding. To "faith" is to not be content with naive credulity, and certainly not with accepting without thought. The writer of the letter to the Hebrews stated that faith did not ignore or bypass evidence, but counted on it (Hebrews 11:1). Faithing will prompt us to reflect carefully on our experience, on the experience of others as reported, on the scriptures, on observation of the world around us. Out of such disciplined reflection, we are freed to make commitments consistent with the assurance that God is indeed trustworthy, the fundamental reality for our world. Faith then provides the environment in which we attempt to structure our convictions into a coherent whole and to express them in language that embodies our understanding.

Sometimes faith is understood as trustfully accepting whatever is offered as authoritative. While "accepting faith" may have some merit, it is "inquiring faith"[4] that provides the dynamic for the theological venture. Paul Edwards's discussion of the role of faith in understanding the world suggests that faith has more to do with wonderment than with acceptance, with "constructive doubt" rather than facile assent:

Revelation cannot exist in a closed society. We must seriously question the validity of our past interpretations and responses—we must doubt in order to wonder—so that new revealings of Christ's love can be meaningful.... To prevent the wonder by rejecting the doubt is a fatal error.[5]

The Will to Dialogue

Although the term "dialogue" has suffered from excessive and superficial use in recent years, the concept and the practice to which it refers remain intensely valuable. In theological discourse it is virtually irreplaceable. However, beyond the mere technical description of the process, it is the spirit in which conversation takes place that makes for effectiveness. Dialogue depends on mutual respect, on the willingness both to speak and to listen, and on the avoidance of the various stratagems by which people often hope to gain the advantage in warfare. Here I am reminded of the description of "being positive" in the *Devil's Dictionary*: being convinced at the top of one's voice.

Speaking and listening are both skills that require some deliberate practice. The original Latin sense of the word "conversation" implied living together and talking together. By contrast, many so-called conversations are monologues. Even if I avoid the impulse to interrupt another, I may be patiently waiting until the other has finished—because civility demands it—before saying exactly what I would have said in the first place. If I do listen intently, it might well be to seize the inept word or false phrase to interrupt and destroy. To listen is to give one's whole self, for the moment, to strive to understand both the statements and the intent behind them, and to be flexible to pursue the conversation where it most fruitfully leads. The Doctrine and Covenants statement cited at the outset of this chapter describes a process that respects both the formality and spirit of dialogue.

The dialogue process gives equal respect, and as far as possible equal freedom, for each participant to be heard. Those who take part will assume the basic human decency of others, and resist the lure of innuendo ("That's the typical attitude of conservatives.") or to intimidation ("Are you trying to tell me...?"). People can become so embroiled in the passion of dialogue, and so intent on preserving both their point of view and their status, that they give way to fanaticism, or blind devotion to their cause. Dialogue can be short-circuited in so many ways that individuals who lack self-confidence will often avoid conversation rather than enter into it, especially if they are in the presence of those thought to be experts. Nevertheless, in the community of the church and in the search for truth, dialogue is so foundational that it must be preserved at virtually all costs. Arguments are rarely "won" in the course of debate. People will rarely admit "defeat" but will generally resolve to argue more effectively on future occasions. But relationships can be irreparably damaged when the spirit of dialogue is neglected.

---

3. Paul Edwards suggests that in the spirit of "constructive doubt" we should seriously question past interpretations and responses, impelled by a sense of wonder. Discuss and evaluate this position. How does this notion relate to your concept of faith, especially "inquiring faith" as contrasted to obedient assent?

4. How many groups do you participate in, religious or otherwise, that provide some opportunity for dialogue? Do you feel that the dialogue is grounded in the principles described above? Would you add other positive aids to dialogue? What helps you to feel most comfortable in dialogue settings? Least comfortable?

Going Deeper

The ability to go below the surface, to refuse to be satisfied with superficial explanations, is significant for the theologian. This will be important for one's own theological understanding. It will be doubly important for those who find themselves in the position of or with the responsibility to interpret the faith for others. Frequently individuals seek help in the form of answers, or solutions, or at least mature perspectives, to searching questions. Not infrequently these occur in the midst of difficult circumstances which have arisen to confront hurting people. Superficial responses will not suffice and may indeed add to the burden.

What response might be made to the harried person who asks: "Does God answer my prayers?" The apparently simple question arises from genuine need on the part of the inquirer and merits the most careful response we can give. A grieving parent asks: "Why did God allow my child to die?" I must admit that I have heard too many answers to that cry for help that neither stand the test of time, nor the dictates of reason, and certainly not the truth of the gospel. Indeed, if we were to be brutally candid, we would be justified in saying that malpractice suits could be brought against "religious authorities" no less than against a medical practitioner or any other professional meeting the public as an expert. For our own sakes, even more so the welfare of those who look for assistance, thoughtful and disciplined study is critical.

Certainly there will be questions for which no answer exists, no matter how deeply pondered, at least at the present time. Under these circumstances it is acceptable to confess ignorance, while at the same time deriving some assurance from the fact that we have made, and are making, every effort to understand matters that impinge so intimately on life experience. Better by far to share one's ongoing search with a seeker than to claim to know when it would be more appropriate to stand humbly before the mystery. However, despite the foregoing, I am persuaded that persistent and diligent searching is rewarded with assurance, if not with answers. This may come to us in the form of hints, nuances, or shadowy intimations of truth, but they prove sufficient for the present time and for the journey and may safely be shared with a fellow traveler.

In this matter dialogue is especially helpful. I have sometimes found myself under the illusion that I had reached as sound an answer as was possible, only to be surprised and deepened in my understanding in the course of such dialogue, even from the most unexpected of sources. So convinced am I of this fact that I have found it highly valuable to provoke informal, albeit intentional conversation whenever possible with people who might have something to contribute. I cannot afford the assumption—which is a form of idolatry—that nobody can help me in my inadequacy. Moreover, schedules and demands on time become so consuming that unless the informal occasions are manufactured they will not happen.

Speaking Generally

The ability to generalize, or to form abstractions, is valuable for the theologian. Although specific instances may provide the data, it is in abstractions that the truth is stated. Specific situations, based on observation, may be incomplete, partly obscured by the context, or clouded by prejudice—vagrant opinions without visible means of support. It will be necessary to move beyond anecdote (concrete particular instances), as interesting as they might be, to general principles drawn from these particulars. The abstractions should emerge, not only from the observation or experience of one person, but from the experience of many people in widely differing circumstances. My friend, after an unpleasant divorce, asked God to lead her to another marriage partner, and "Henry" came onto the scene. From this she has reached the generalization that God will provide marriage partners when we ask in faith. Another acquaintance came to the conclusion that "God will provide" based on two fortunate "bail-outs," and then came to grief when he assumed that God would provide in a third situation.

5. Do you find yourself wrestling with questions for which the "answers" seem to elude you? Can you share these questions with other members of your group? How do you cope with that situation in the meantime? Are there occasions when it seems critical for you to possess an answer? How does your congregation help you?

6. Identify some generalizations that you believe have been made on inadequate grounds. Did this pose a potential problem or disillusionment for those reaching conclusions on this basis? If you had opportunity and thought it helpful, how would you respond to my friend's conclusion regarding the divine role in arranging marriage partners?

Yielding Gracefully

Rare is the person who proves to be "right" in a religious discussion. Indeed, as Joseph Smith III believed, there will be many matters in which it is impossible to state with final authority who is right and who is wrong in a debated matter. However, there will be instances when a difference of opinion can be resolved by the appeal to demonstrable facts. In such cases it is important for the preservation of a good spirit in theological dialogue for a person to be able to yield gracefully, confess error, and give credit where it belongs. If the overriding concern is for the truth, and not for the preservation of one's dignity or status, then it should be freeing to the person who can yield gracefully, and will contribute to further opportunities for dialogue in the future.

The Spirit of Tolerance

Most dictionaries provide a range of definitions for the term "tolerance." Maurice Draper has been helpful in pointing to the particular relevance of two of these meanings for the theological process.[6] In the first place, and probably most obvious, tolerance refers to freedom from bigotry, the maintenance of a fair and objective attitude exhibited by individuals in their relationships with others. The need for tolerance in theological discussion, especially in those circumstances where tolerance may be strained, is apparent.

There is another application of the term that is equally important, having to do with the dictionary definition of "permissive range of variation in a dimension of an object." Thus we might refer to the tolerance of a length of plastic pipe, speaking of its ability to accommodate certain demands of pressure or temperature while retaining its ability to serve the purpose for which it was fashioned. In the same way, it is appropriate to consider, both in personal conversation and in explorations of the corporate body, what the bearable limits of inquiry are. While strictly impersonal criteria might suggest that there are no limits, pastoral sensitivity might confess that any person or group has limits on the ability to withstand assaults on their ideas. While this consideration should not become a rationalization for avoiding new ventures in theology, the long-term concern for the health of the body should be taken into account. Nevertheless, "Our people are not ready to deal with that yet" should not mean "I feel uncomfortable with that idea myself and would just as soon avoid it."

If a person has taken a long period of time to come to certain insights, it would hardly be fair or considerate to expect another person, totally unexposed to the idea, to feel comfortable in dealing with it at short notice. For obvious reasons educational programs are designed to permit an orderly and sequential exposure to ideas or skills. Incoming freshmen are not judged on their ability to handle postgraduate language study, or any other advanced study, although immature professors may sometimes find personal gratification in shocking freshmen with their daring pronouncements.

Although a "graded curriculum" attempts to provide an orderly sequence for younger members, adults are not exposed to ideas in the same orderly fashion that colleges can ensure. However, the need to recognize and practice tolerance in this sense is just as important. Otherwise the ultimate objective of dialogue—that is, the optimum growth of the maximum number of people—is defeated, all in the name of the pursuit of truth.

---

7. Some people are of the opinion that the church in recent years has exceeded the limits of tolerance, both with respect to the range of ideas that have been discussed and the rate at which they have been introduced. Do you think this is a justified opinion? If so, what ideas do you think have come to the attention of the membership "before their time"? What ideas do you think might still be premature for the membership to consider?

8. Given the reality that, among any group of church members, individuals are at different stages in their journey, what steps can be taken to ensure that each person is helped to encounter new ideas without being overwhelmed or threatened? What obligations, if any, rest with members who feel very comfortable with these same ideas? Are there some ideas currently under consideration with which you feel uncomfortable? How do you deal with this situation?

Examining the Examiner

A notion that once prevailed unchallenged, but which now seems incredibly naive, was that the search for scientific truth could be impartial or objective, whereas other fields, such as religion, were saturated with subjectivity. We are now only too aware that in every field of human inquiry, the searcher is a significant factor in the equation. M. Scott Peck, in writing of the need to revise our conceptual maps (previously cited in this study), insists that the process is one that calls for total dedication to the truth. However, the seeker does not bring a completely objective self to the study. Perceptions about ourselves, prejudices, self-interests, motivations lingering below the surface, will exercise a decisive effect on what truth is "discovered." So Peck asks:

> What does a life of total dedication to the truth mean? It means, first of all, a life of continuous and never-ending stringent self-examination. We know the world only through our relationship to it. Therefore, to know the world, we must not only examine it but we must simultaneously examine the examiner.... A life of total dedication to the truth also means a life of willingness to be personally challenged. The only way that we can be certain that our map of reality is valid is to expose it to the criticism and challenge of other map-makers. Otherwise we live in a closed system.[7]

Engagement or Detachment

Theology is not a pastime for people who are simply intrigued by a challenge. Nor is it intended to provide the battleground for those who need to feel vindicated in argument or superior in intellect. Rather, theology is a serious and practical effort to reach an understanding of our faith for the journey. For this cause, the attitude of engagement is called for, rather than one of detachment. Theology is not a subject, in the narrow sense of the word, something to be inspected, prodded, examined under a microscope, mastered. It is a venture from which a sense of wonderment and humility is never far removed.

The quality, or gift, that underlies all other skills and disciplines for theology, is the spirit of commitment to truth, and to the One whose truth it is that we endeavor to perceive.

9. Peck suggests it is a temptation to avoid truth or reality when it is painful. Have you experienced such pain in your journey? How did you deal with it? Did you find help from any source?

10. Discuss Peck's two principles related to dedication to truth: the willingness to undergo self-examination and the willingness to be challenged by others. Do you think that to some extent the church might have provided a closed system in its claim of former years to be the exclusive possessor of truth and authority?

Activities for the Reader

A. Review the study resources in your home library. List these by category: dictionaries, commentaries, concordances, encyclopedias, handbooks on specific subjects, religious histories, books on theology in general, and books on specific subjects. Are there noticeable gaps or omissions in your listing? Which do you use most? How do you mark your books to make the most effective use of them? How can you provide for a growing range of resources?

B. Make a list, as completely as you are able, of the formal or informal theological discussions in which you have been a participant over the past month. Identify topics and settings. Which do you think were the most productive for you? Why? The least productive? Why? What do you think can be done, if anything, to improve the quality of such theological discussions in your congregation?

Notes

1. Anthony Chvala-Smith, *Core Values of the RLDS Church*, booklet in the *Congregational Leaders Handbook*, Communities of Joy, B-1 (Independence, Missouri: Herald House, 1994).
2. George Santayana, *The Life of Reason*, Vol. 2.
3. *The Christian Century*, source not located.
4. Paul M. Edwards, *Inquiring Faith: An Exploration in Religious Education* (Independence, Missouri: Herald House, 1967).
5. Ibid., 35.
6. Maurice L. Draper, unpublished notes titled, "Limits on Tolerance" (1995).
7. M. Scott Peck, *The Road Less Traveled* (New York: Simon and Schuster, 1978), 51.

History Preview

Indicate whether you believe each of the following statements to be true or false. The answers will be found on p. 204.

1. Section 156 of the Doctrine and Covenants (1984) was approved by a closer margin than any other section.   T   F

2. All of the following have been members of the First Presidency of the original Restoration Church (1830–44) or the RLDS Church: Israel A. Smith, Sidney Rigdon, Jesse Gause, Duane Couey, F. Henry Edwards.   T   F

3. Joseph Smith's final viewpoint regarding celestial glory was that only those who had been baptized into the Restored church, or had received proxy baptism for the dead, could be heirs of this glory.   T   F

4. Women were not permitted to vote on matters presented to the General Conference until granted that right in 1868.   T   F

5. Joseph Smith's account of the "grove experience" (often referred to as the "first vision") as it appears in the first few pages of *Church History* was the account with which most members who came into the early Restoration movement were familiar.   T   F

6. With the possible exception of a First Presidency, all of the formal priesthood officers found in the Restoration movement (apostles, high priests, bishops, seventy, evangelists, elders, priests, teachers, and deacons) also existed in the early Jerusalem church.   T   F

7. The first members of the Council of Twelve in the Restoration were chosen through a revelatory document presented by Joseph Smith.   T   F

8. The function of bishops in the New Testament church was as financial officers, similar to their function in the Restoration church.   T   F

9. The first edition of what was called Joseph Smith's New Translation of the Bible (subsequently known as the Inspired Version) was, except for versification and punctuation, a precise copy of the manuscript delivered to the church by Emma Smith.   T   F

10. The concept of the land of America as the New Jerusalem, or Zion, was introduced by revelations brought to the early members of the Restoration movement.   T   F

Chapter 9

Like Thieves in the Night

"I don't understand it. If the fullness of the gospel was restored through the Restoration, why do members of the church want to keep introducing new ideas and ways of doing things? This attempt to permit variations in the way we state the Communion prayers is just one more example."

—A delegate to the 1996 World Conference

"For they are a rebellious people, faithless children...who say to the seers 'Do not see,' and to the prophets, 'Do not prophesy to us what is right; speak to us...smooth things, prophesy illusions,...let us hear no more about the Holy One of Israel.'"

—Isaiah 30:9–11 (NRSV)

The Comfort of the Familiar

It is appropriate at this point to take up in more detail a theme introduced in chapter 2: the notion that ideas and understandings that eventually become accepted are almost invariably resisted at the time of their introduction. Such ideas are condemned as threatening to the social fabric, destructive of decency and tradition, and heretical subversions of eternal truth. Ideas and practices of such value to the march of history must insinuate themselves into the public consciousness "like thieves in the night," generally advocated by a small minority of individuals (perhaps even a minority of one) who will bear the condemnation and hostility of their fellows in the process.

No field of knowledge or inquiry appears to have escaped this tendency. When universal suffrage was first proposed, the disintegration of society was prophesied. The early proponents of women's suffrage encountered not only scorn and hostility, but also the prediction that the extension of the vote to women would mean the end of dignity and intelligence in the political process. When advocates of labor reform proposed a ten-hour daily limit on the employment of young children in mines and factories, employers bemoaned the undermining of the industrial system. The notion that Gentiles might be acceptable in the primitive church prompted outrage on the part of the established membership and led to a council at Jerusalem to test this dangerous and heretical idea. It would appear that there is a powerful appeal, as well as comfort, in the preservation of the familiar.

When the prophet Isaiah realized that Jerusalem, during the reign of Hezekiah (705–701 B.C.), looked to traditional support from Egypt to resist the Assyrian threat, he accused them of preferring "smooth things" promised by the prophets to trusting in the future of God. In the very early part of his public ministry, Jesus challenged his hearers to beware of the comfort of the familiar: "Ye have heard that it has been said of them of old time.... But I say unto you."[1] It may have been fear of the unfamiliar, or lack of maturity, or a combination of both, that prompted Jesus to say to his disciples toward the end of his ministry: "I have yet many things to say unto you, but ye cannot bear them now."[2]

Hostages to History

Certainly the foregoing is intended neither to dismiss the familiar and traditional, nor to venerate the new and innovative. Just as the antiquity of an idea or practice is no guarantee of its validity, so the novelty of an idea offers no assurance of its truthfulness. We are well advised to "try" ideas as well as "spirits" (see I John 4:1). This will alert us to the fact that new truth does not always enter the world, or the church, with a fanfare of trumpets and ready acceptance. It also serves to remind us that every new notion, or fad, may not stand the tests of time and careful appraisal. Some church members were intrigued with the "hollow earth" theory that enjoyed a fleeting appeal in the 1960s and early 1970s. From time to time considerable excitement has been aroused by "reports" of the resting place of ancient records alleged to have a connection with the Book of Mormon. There will always be a number of Christians, as in the present time, who hail each new prophecy of the impending end of the world as if it were a novel idea in the long history of Christianity. There is no shame in declaring ourselves to be Latter Day Saints so long as we are aware of the failure of previous attempts to construct a literal timetable of world history, invariably announcing the imminent end.

It is at this point that a healthy and informed awareness of our history proves its value. As suggested earlier, the natural inclination is to believe that the church has always believed and acted as it believes and acts within our living memory. It is not only, as Santayana claimed, that those who cannot remember their history are condemned to repeat it. Perhaps more importantly, those whose memory extends no further back than their own lifetime have no appreciation for the fact that change has been a constant element in our past. They may therefore fear any change that confronts us in our present situation. For instance, members of the church who casually approve the vote of females in our conferences may not realize that this was a hard-won freedom, emerging from the spirited debate of the 1868 General Conference. A resolution offered in 1873, proposing a return to the status quo, was defeated after "lengthy and spirited discussion." Yet today it is a change generally accepted without thought.

More recently, the confusion of some delegates at the 1996 World Conference over the church's position on "literal" or "plenary" revelation might have been eased had they been aware of the church's decision stated more than a century ago[3] and affirmed by Joseph Smith III under oath while giving evidence in the Temple Lot Suit. Whether these actions were correct or not—and the church has denied that it has the authority to make any infallible judgment in such matters—the church has long assumed a position that is still not known to many church members. In this matter, as well as in many others, we are indeed either "hostages to history" because of our ignorance of it, or people who can be blessed by their historical awareness in the consideration of new issues that arise.

A sense of history, then, preserves us from the arrogance of assuming that everything of importance or truthfulness has already been thought of or revealed to us. On the other hand such a familiarity with history saves us from the embarrassment of having to admit that ideas that at first were opposed are now accepted and valid, and over the course of time may have become deeply embedded in the faith of the people.

1. Identify an idea or development with which you felt some discomfort or uncertainty when it was first introduced. Why did you experience this discomfort? What, if anything, helped you to overcome your uncertainty, or does it still persist? Did you find yourself supported by other members as you struggled with this change?

2. In your experience in the church, can you recall ideas that seemed to stimulate considerable excitement or anticipation, but which do not seem to have

led to anything fruitful? Do you think there may be such ideas in the contemporary Christian world that may not stand the test of time? Can you give reasons for your opinion?

Substance or Preference

The purpose of this chapter, then, is to identify certain ideas or practices that were first seen as "innovations," examine the circumstances in which they arose, and note how they have become part of the tradition. Before proceeding to specific cases, it might be helpful to suggest that new ideas and practices may be understood as either matters of substance—having an identifiable impact on the faith and theology of the church—or matters of preference, arising from the feelings or taste of the members.

Of course, opinions may vary regarding where any particular issue will fall, and the boundary between the two might not always be clear-cut. As early as 1781 the Englishman Robert Raikes was responsible for the introduction of the Sunday School movement, and in 1824 the American Sunday School Union was established. However, the introduction of religious education was not achieved for youth and children in the church without considerable question as to whether this was consistent with the purpose of the gospel. Some strongly defended the position that this responsibility rested with parents (as proposed in Doctrine and Covenants 68:4a–c), and for some time the Sunday School organization was administered independently of congregational structure. Again, when the question arose as to whether the elders should answer requests for administrations if the individuals involved had sought medical advice, some insisted the matter had a direct bearing on the belief regarding laying on of hands for the sick and could be considered a test of faith. Joseph Smith III responded to the matter in a *Herald* editorial in such a way as to advise moderation and to defuse the heated debate on the matter.[4]

The same kind of difference of opinion was voiced over dispensing with the common cup during the Communion service in favor of using individual cups. For some it was essentially a question of sensible hygiene; for others it struck at the very heart of the sacrament. Congregations have been known to experience serious tension over the matter of the color of the new carpet for the sanctuary, or the particular make of organ to be installed for worship. During President Frederick Madison Smith's administration, debate was stirred by his effort to separate celebration of the Communion from the prayer and testimony meeting. In more recent years the issue of the "fitness" of certain styles of congregational worship, or of certain instruments, or of specific details in the serving of the Lord's Supper, or again of specific terms of reference to God have sparked debate over the impact of these issues on the essence of the gospel. It is a matter of record that the energy and heat provoked by debate has not necessarily borne any relation to the magnitude of the issue involved.

---

3. Can you personally, or the class together, recall matters that might have stirred debate in the congregation? Can you rank these in order of significance? Are there some of these items that you would define as matters of substance, and others as matters of taste or preference? If you can recall no such instances of debate, what explanation can you offer?

The Boldness of the Founding Prophet

It is instructive to note Joseph Smith's apparent freedom to develop and express new understandings, even when they involved the revision of ideas he had previously held. In most instances these are reflected in revisions that he made in the original text of the scriptures with which he had been working. In addition to the revisions written onto the printer's manuscript of the Book of Mormon and subsequently embodied in the 1830 first edition, Joseph continued to refine the text of the 1837 Kirtland and 1840 Nauvoo editions. While many of these are grammatical or stylistic, a number reflect a rethinking and restatement of the original text.

Similar manuscript evidence demonstrates a readiness on Joseph's part to reconsider and, if necessary, revise the text of what came to be known as the Inspired Version and of the documents selected for inclusion in the 1835 edition of the Doctrine and Covenants. Some of these may be primarily matters that provoke interest, such as writing Jesse Gause out of history in favor of Frederick G. Williams (Doctrine and Covenants Section 80). Others are of greater substance, such as the change in the description of Oliver Cowdrey's "gift" (Doctrine and Covenants 8:3b–f) or the reversal of the procedure for handling the consecration of property (Doctrine and Covenants 42:8–11). However significant the changes are judged to be, they throw important light on the manner of Joseph's dealing with the text. Richard Howard's *Restoration Scriptures: A Study of Their Textual Development* (Second Edition, 1995) provides a comprehensive analysis of the process.

Both Richard Howard and I recall the distress and resentment some members reflected when this subject, along with the accompanying manuscript data, was first presented in field seminars. For many members, evidence that Joseph had modified his first draft of the scriptural text appeared to bring his authority as a prophet into question. Others interpreted this data positively to reflect the process of growth in understanding under the influence of the guiding Spirit. When church historian Charles Davies responded to the question: "What was the 'gift of Aaron' mentioned in Doctrine and Covenants 8?" he explained that this was a change from the original wording "the gift of working with the rod," and referred to Oliver Cowdery's reputation for skill in using the witch-hazel stick. He then went on to state:

> I believe a study of the Book of Commandments (1833) in comparison with the Doctrine and Covenants at this point indicates a development of Joseph Smith's understandings between 1830 and the publication in 1835. When his concepts changed, he revised the text to conform.[5]

While it would be presumptuous to claim to know the prophet's mind, at least one incident does serve to throw light on the matter under consideration. This has been referred to in the History Preview, concerning an experience reported by Joseph Smith during a meeting of the First Presidency in Kirtland Temple on January 21, 1836:

> The heavens were opened upon us, and I beheld the celestial kingdom of God, and the glory thereof, whether in the body or without I cannot tell.... I saw...my father and mother, my brother Alvin, that has long since slept, and marveled how it was that he had obtained an inheritance in that kingdom, seeing that he had departed this life before the Lord had set his hand to gather Israel the second time, and had not been baptized for the remission of sins. Thus came the voice of the Lord unto me, saying—"All who have died without a knowledge of this gospel, who would have received it if they had been permitted to tarry, shall be heirs of the celestial kingdom of God; also all that shall die henceforth without a knowledge of it, who would have received it with all their hearts, shall be heirs of that kingdom...."[6]

The incident as described reveals Joseph Smith's ability to be surprised by insights that ran contrary to those he had previously held, even insights rooted in significant revelatory experience, as in what is now Section 76 of the Doctrine and Covenants. If the term "disjunctive revelation" serves any useful purpose, then it may describe such a process as disclosed by the founding prophet's own experience and work with the scriptural text.

4. Charles Davies stated that when Joseph Smith's concepts changed, he revised the text of what he had written to conform. How does this help you understand the process of revelation? Does it have any significance for your own continuing growth?
5. The term "disjunctive revelation" has been used to describe revelatory insights that are genuinely new, representing a break with what has been previously understood. Can such experiences (such as underlying the provision permitting the ordination of women) indeed be genuine? If so, what is the prospect of similar "disjunctive" insights occurring in the future?

Precept upon Precept

The question raised by the perplexed Conference delegate is indeed understandable: Why does this process of change or projected change seem endless, and how can we be sure that the changes are valid? The answers may not be assuring or comfortable: there may well be no end in our lifetime or beyond, and there is, in the words of Joseph Smith III, "no absolute tribunal" that can decide the truth or error of those changes. People of good conscience may argue strenuously for or against any specific change, and cite scriptural "proof" or spiritual confirmation to vindicate their positions. But the venture is always one of faith.

Issues debated and decisions made in remote time, or before our own lifetime, may be relatively easy to live with. The decisions to admit gentile converts to the church, to allow women the right to vote at church conferences, or to maintain a waiting stance on baptism for the dead, cause little pain now, although there were many who suffered discomfort at the time, and often for some time afterward. More recent decisions or trends touch us more closely and few are unaffected, whatever their position might be.

In general, new ideas do not develop in isolation from each other but as parts of the broader pattern of belief. This is certainly not to suggest any conspiracy among advocates of change but rather to affirm that any one part of the fabric of belief can hardly be evaluated without other parts being impacted. Thus there has been a gradual though consistent movement over the past half-century to reexamine broad issues relating to the church, its nature, authority, mission, relation to other churches, and role in salvation. To provide some historical perspective the following brief statement, made in response to an inquiring member and published in *Question Time*, represents with reasonable completeness the predominant view of church members in the period preceding 1955:

> Our church stands unique among churches in that it holds a system of gospel truth and ordinances distinct from all others, which system was revealed directly from heaven in original purity and fullness, in substitution of the perverse systems which have arisen since the days of the apostles. To administer that primitive gospel restored in latter days, the Lord delivered from heaven to chosen men by angelic hands the holy priesthood, giving them power and authority to officiate in the preaching of the word, the administering of its ordinances, and in the government of the affairs of the church, which he made the repository and administrator of that gospel.[7]

I am old enough to remember the church of that period, to have heard virtually universally that interpretation of the church, and to have supported myself, though with increasing discomfort after my early twenties. I have also experienced, on occasion too directly for comfort, the struggles of recent years. Some members have interpreted the various trends that have become increasingly preeminent as part of an intentional movement to abandon traditional gospel truths, to blunt the unique role and authority of the Reorganization, and to manifest a liberal desire to sacrifice treasured beliefs in order to move toward the mainstream of Protestant orthodoxy. From a nonmember's perspective, Larry Conrad has described the uncertainty and confusion that resulted from the perceived failure to connect the new trends in thinking with the treasured images, symbols, and stories of the Restoration: "This theological vacuum has simply been too much to bear for some persons raised with traditional Reorganization views of church history and exclusive claims to theological and salvific truth."[8]

The ultimate judgment about such changes, and the motivations prompting them, are matters of opinion and expressions of faith. People have a tendency to accuse protagonists of improper or impure motives, while claiming for themselves only the purest of intentions. In this respect, the admonition offered so emphatically by Joseph Smith III after fifty years of presidency in the church again becomes critical, that differences should be expressed in a free and mutually respectful atmosphere.

---

6. To what extent do you think Joseph Smith III's advice about the manner of conducting discussion or debate in matters of difference has been observed or neglected? To what extent has the church been helped or injured by the predominant styles of dialogue?

The issues have been highly significant. At the heart of the inquiry have been questions about the nature of the Restoration and its relationship to the broad sweep of Christian history. Traditionally, members emphatically based the church's authority and right to exist on the claim that a complete apostasy from the faith had been inherited by all other Christian churches. Roy Cheville raised questions about this interpretation of history in his 1962 book, *Did the Light Go Out?* In

Cheville's view, the "nature and the integrity" of a God who could completely abandon the world to "go on a long recess" had to be called into question. The appeal to a mathematical formula based on dubious interpretation of scripture exacerbated the issue:

> I was told that the year A.D. 570 marked the coming of the "apostasy" or departure from the light of the Christian gospel. It appeared as if God or someone had put a finger on the light switch that particular year and had turned out the light all over the world. (An interpretation of Revelation 12:14 had suggested the number 1260 which, subtracted from A.D. 1830, gave the year.) ...For more than twenty-five years I have been thinking about these centuries.[9]

The question raised—and implicitly answered—by Cheville was addressed more directly in the book *Exploring the Faith*, published as the work of the Basic Beliefs Committee, which had been engaged in the project of preparing a statement of belief for more than a decade. In an extended comment on the paragraph titled "The Church," the committee offered the following:

> It would be wrong to say that the church at any time was totally bad or that it had no authority.... The community of believers has continued in some sense from the days of Christ to our present time. In fact, one could hardly see how there could be any church on earth at all if at any time after the ascension of Christ the life and spirit of the Christian community had been totally blotted out. There is a real sense in which we must recognize our indebtedness to the continuing Christian community through which the knowledge, spirit, and life of the incarnation have been preserved and engendered even into our own generation....
>
> Our biggest danger is that we assume that because we are the Church of Jesus Christ and have authority growing out of our experience with God, no other authority to represent God exists outside our own fellowship.[10]

While the Basic Beliefs Committee was preparing the final text of its statement for publication, similar themes had been developed in a series of articles—erroneously described as "position papers"—written by the Department of Religious Education. In the absence of any clear theological guidelines, the First Presidency had appointed a committee at the request of the department to enter into dialogue concerning foundations for a projected new curriculum, and the papers had been prepared as guides for the ensuing discussions.

Almost two decades after the appearance of Cheville's book, the broad questions of the nature and mission of the church were addressed in January 1979 in a series of presentations for discussion by the World Church appointees. The purpose of the gathering, called by the First Presidency, was to move toward some consensus in the missionary witness of the church and to lay the foundation for the Faith to Grow program of the approaching decade. The paper titled "The Identity of the Church" included the following:

> The church is blessed with authority. It has the full measure of authority appropriate to its life and witness.... An unfortunate and erroneous concept about the nature of authority is that only one organized church institution at a time may have authority to represent God.... It is our faith and understanding of God that no available means or opportunity to save and bless the people of the world will be overlooked. We believe also that God's Holy Spirit works with persons and groups in ways we may not presently discern.... Our faith in the majesty and power of that revelation would be diminished immeasurably if we perceived the ongoing authoritative ministry of Jesus Christ as being confined to our day and sect.[11]

At the same time, a related line of inquiry was pursuing a direction that was viewed by some as undermining the authority of the priesthood and the church. Traditionally it had been seen as important to claim identity between the organizational structure of the New Testament and the restored church, with both including the same ordained offices. A more careful reading of the New Testament, along with greater exposure to early Christian literature—notably the writings of Clement, Ignatius, Polycarp, and the *Didache* (or *The Teaching of the Twelve*

Apostles)—painted a picture that was more faithful to history. In this respect, the Basic Beliefs Committee wrote: "The Bible is not a comprehensive source book of information about the history of the early Christian church. We ought not to read into the early Christian church the counterpart of our own organization and structure in any detailed way.[12]

---

7. Discuss the change in our understanding of apostasy described here. In your opinion, does this do violence to scripture or weaken the right of the church to exist as an authoritative body and witness of Christ in the world?
8. Consider the change in our view of the church's priesthood structure, as compared with that of the early Christian church. Do you believe the authority or effectiveness of the priesthood is lessened by this more recent position?

The explorations described here, and others that have ensued both informally and through the formal actions of World Conference, have embraced a wide spectrum of developments that have surely tested the faith and courage of the Saints, and would seem to support the basic thesis of this book, that theology is indeed a hazardous enterprise. The capacity of the church to bear such a wide range of developments as listed below will be seen as either encouraging or distressing, depending upon one's point of view:
- the recovery of emphasis on doctrines central to the faith but often associated with Protestantism: grace, justification
- the emphasis on the traditional view (though not widely recognized as such) regarding plenary inspiration and its implications for a doctrine of scripture

- the authority of the church with respect to other Christian bodies
- the use of the Christian calendar, adding Lent and Advent to the traditionally accepted observance of Christmas and Easter
- the opening of the ordained offices of ministry to women
- the greater use of liturgical elements in worship, such as responsive readings and the wider variety of worship forms and styles
- recognition of the priesthood structure of the church as essentially a development of the Restoration
- the adoption of a modified open Communion
- the ongoing study of the conditions of membership
- the increased disposition to participate in ecumenical ventures
- a stronger emphasis on Zion as an informing symbol of the church's mission in the world, in place of the literal view of a specific community with a particular geographic reference.

More Light and Truth?

The processes of evaluation and change will most likely continue. If the editorial revisions carried out by Joseph Smith Jr. on the manuscript of the Book of Mormon are included, then this process reaches back to the earliest years of the Restoration movement, and even before the actual organization of the church. There is no reason to believe we are blessed with the gift of foresight and are able to foresee comfortably what those developments might be, any more than it was possible to predict in 1830, 1844, 1860, or 1950 the precise nature and form of the church to come.

The search for new understandings has rarely, if ever, been prompted by the desire to parade scholarship, win fame or prestige, or shatter idols. Ample evidence suggests that the exploration into new thought, while it might have appeared to some as the venture of "thieves in the night," has been powerfully driven by the restless and sometimes painful longing to be faithful to the call of the gospel. Precisely when such longings were beginning to stir in the recent half-century, F. Henry Edwards commented on the tension between the old and the new, between the established traditions and the unchartered "new highlands of understanding" (cited in chapter 6), which necessarily called the faithful into the future. Edwards's book *Fundamentals*, first published in 1936 (with a fourth edition "extensively revised" in 1958), though deceptively innocent in its title, was a forerunner in lifting up new understandings and was criticized by many as the work of a young rebel.

Unnerving as it might seem, the challenges to further exploration are likely to persist.

Activities for the Reader

A. List on a separate sheet, or in your workbook, the changes listed toward the end of this chapter, with the exception of the ongoing study of conditions of membership. Then state briefly for each one (a) how you felt about the change at the time it was first discussed or introduced, and (b) how you feel about it now. Finally, write a single sentence summing up your feelings about these developments.

B. Select one of the following:
   - What changes, if any, would you like to see introduced into the church in the future? Choose one of these and state briefly in writing what you believe the response would be if the matter were proposed in (a) your congregation, (b) your district or stake, (c) the World Conference.
   - What changes, if any, would you like to see reversed in the church of the future, so that the situation returned to the way it was formerly? Select one and state what you believe the response would be if the matter were proposed in (a) your congregation, (b) your district or stake, (c) the World Conference.

Notes

1. Matthew 5:21–22, 27–28, 33–34 (KJV); 5:23–24, 29–30, 37–38 (IV).
2. John 16:12.
3. General Conference Resolution 308:7 (approved April 1886).
4. *Saints' Herald* 44, no. 6 (February 10, 1897): 81–82.
5. Charles Davies, *Question Time*, Vol. 2 (Independence, Missouri: Herald House, 1967), 49.
6. *Church History*, 2:16.
7. *Question Time*, Vol. 1 (Independence, Missouri: Herald House, 1955), 337. The questions and answers included in this first volume were selected from those published in the *Herald* between 1949 and 1953. Both the kind of questions asked and the answers offered make an interesting contrast with those appearing in the second volume, published twelve years later.
8. Larry W. Conrad, "Dissent Among Dissenters" in Roger D. Launius and W. B. "Pat" Spillman, eds., *Let Contention Cease* (Independence, Missouri: Graceland/Park Press, 1991), 223.
9. Roy A. Cheville, *Did the Light Go Out?* (Independence, Missouri: Herald House, 1962), Foreword.
10. Basic Beliefs Committee, *Exploring the Faith,* (Independence, Missouri: Herald House, 1970), 130–131. Readers should also study the chapter on "The Church" (143–171) in the 1987 edition.
11. "Identity of the Church," an unpublished paper presented at a conference of World Church appointees (January 1979), 12–13.
12. *Exploring the Faith* (1970 edition), 131.

Chapter 10

Through a Glass Darkly

"The reason we have so much confusion and disbelief is that people substitute the words of men for the word of God. God has spoken to us directly by revelation, so that we may trust his words as pure and uncontaminated by any human influence."

— Stated during a discussion on revelation

"We do not consider it [the Inspired Version] infallible, nor do we consider the Bible infallible. We do not consider anything that passes through human hands to be infallible. We do not believe in the plenary inspiration of the Bible; we hold that everything which passes through human hands is fallible."

— Joseph Smith III, giving evidence during the Temple Lot Suit

It would be of supreme comfort to most human beings to know that there is available to us some source of ultimate and unquestionable truth, beyond any shadow of doubt or clever argument, dependable for all times and in every circumstance. In a world of confusion, with so many competing voices, such a "word" would be more precious than diamonds. For many Christians this oasis of certainty is found in the Bible, so that the doctrine of the innerancy of scripture becomes the point where the faith of others is submitted to the litmus test. Some theological seminaries will only accept students who have signed a statement witnessing their acceptance of this position.

Nevertheless, despite its high regard for scripture and its testimony to the ongoing power of revelation in the life of the body, the church has declined to invest its security in any insistence on a view of literal inspiration. Joseph Smith III addressed a familiar theme when he wrote in one of his "Pleasant Chats" in the *Herald*:

> The term "inspired," as qualifying speeches, writings, copies and translations, signifies that the agent employed to speak, to write, to copy, to translate, was commanded, or permitted, delegated or authorized to do that particular work, and was given a sufficient amount of the divine afflatus to fit him for that work; not that said agent lost identity with the human family, with freedom from all earthly imperfection, and spoke, wrote, copied or translated, as the finger of God himself.[1]

The fact is, of course, that every person is part of the human family. There is no way a person can distance himself or herself from that family, either in terms of the imperfections referred to by the president, or from the entire web of human patterns and relationships that constitute life on earth. It is those relationships and patterns, ways of thinking and behaving, that make up who I am. If I am asked to identify myself I respond with much more than my given name, which might in fact convey very little. I do so in ways that locate me in time and space in that family, and that may communicate a great deal about gender, family ties, citizenship, religious affiliation, age, educational background, occupation, and other details deemed appropriate to complete the picture. These are the influences permeating every phase of life that make up my cultural environment, with culture understood as

> the integrated pattern of human behavior that includes thought, speech, action, and artifacts and depends upon man's capacity for learning and transmitting knowledge to succeeding generations: the customary be-

liefs, social forms, and material traits of a racial, religious, or social group.[2]

This chapter resumes the theme briefly treated in chapter 5: each person's participation in a particular cultural environment and the impact of that culture on the individual's theological understanding. Three major questions will be raised: First, to what extent is scripture influenced, if at all, by the cultural background of its authors? Second, how does a person deal with his or her own cultural biases in developing theological understandings? Finally, to what extent may church members be impacted by the cultural values surrounding them, and how will this affect their participation in the larger society?

1. A church member says: "If you can't believe in the Bible, the Book of Mormon, or the Doctrine and Covenants as the very word(s) of God, how can you have any security or trust in God at all?" How would you respond, either in support or reflecting another position?
2. The author of I Timothy wrote, in respect of a certain matter: "the Spirit expressly says." The apostle Paul stated on one occasion that what he wrote was "by way of permission, and not by commandment" (I Corinthians 7:6). What do you consider to be the difference in the authority of these two situations, if any? Give reasons for your opinion.

Culture and Sacred Writ

For some people, to suggest that scripture, or inspired writings or statements, are in any way affected by cultural influences and therefore less than perfect is a grievous error. While human thought and utterance is indeed tainted, the argument runs, inspiration delivers a pure and uncontaminated word of

God, which as such becomes the "iron rod" against all human imperfection. To suggest anything less is to threaten the credibility of scripture and leave human beings powerless on the shifting sands of "man-made" pronouncements. Such a conviction is reflected, for example, in resolutions submitted to the 1986 World Conference that declared scripture (or at least certain parts of it) to be free of cultural influence, and took the position that no cultural influences would have obstructed God's word had female participation in priesthood been part of the divine purpose.

Nevertheless, it does seem to be difficult for those who insist on the innerancy of scripture to be consistent in their judgments. Some who uphold as universally binding Paul's injunction against women participating in the meetings of the church (I Corinthians 14:34–35) would consider rulings given in the same letter concerning head covering for women (I Corinthians 11:3–10) to be limited in its application. In the same way, as societal standards regarding marriage change, some who insist on the absolute truth of words attributed to Jesus will ignore his statements regarding adultery (Luke 16:23 IV, 16:18 others; Matthew 19:9). It is difficult to discern by what criteria some statements are regarded as universally binding and ultimate, while others are considered time- and culture-bound.

The position taken by Joseph Smith III in court testimony, in statements to the Conference, and in such writings as cited above, adopts a different view: that *all* human expressions, including those considered inspired, will bear the impress of the human agent. Walter Johnson, formerly presiding bishop of the church, supported this point of view:

> Inspiration is conditioned by the background of the individual being inspired. Education, or lack of it; adjustments, or lack of adjustments, to the life of his day; the depth and intensity of religious feeling, cultural and social background will condition the inspiration which is achieved and will be reflected in the interpretation of any inspirational experience.[3]

In discussing the nature of the Book of Mormon, Roy Cheville expressed the conviction that the ideas and wording of the text naturally would reflect Joseph Smith's cultural environment:

> We would expect Joseph Smith to disclose his background and his abilities in his inspired expressions.... [H]e would be affected by the concerns and issues and interests and questions of his times. His was a Bible-minded world, and the Bible was the King James, or Authorized Version. He would use phrases with a Bible flavor. His was a Calvinism-influenced world with some persons favoring and some disfavoring Calvinistic theology. The concerns about predestination, election, depravity of man, infant baptism, or the inability of man to effect his own salvation, the atonement through Jesus Christ, the grace of God would be in his thinking and vocabulary. These would come out in his spoken and written expressions.[4]

Cheville took up this same theme in another study, *The Book of Mormon Speaks for Itself*, written some years later:

> Joseph Smith would use what verbal resources he could mobilize. These would go beyond the usual manner of expression. It would be expected that the language of a farm boy of his background would condition the phrasing and organization of the story of the Book of Mormon.... Joseph Smith's time and environment would ever have influence in his dictating to Oliver Cowdery, his scribe. In the translating would appear the patterns of thinking and phrasing of the translator. The man who speaks for God uses the means at his disposal in the world of his thinking. These would tend to express the doctrinal forms of the time in which Joseph Smith was living.[5]

---

3. Evaluate the positions taken by Walter Johnson and Roy Cheville concerning the impact of an individual's cultural environment on written or verbal statements judged to be inspired. How do their statements relate to the statement made by Joseph Smith III? Discuss the implications of Cheville's comments on your understanding of the Book of Mormon text.

Timeless or Time-bound?

Rather than asking whether any specific passage of writing bears a cultural imprint or not, it may be more helpful to ask: "Does this statement convey positions that were essentially limited to a particular time and place and specific circumstances, or does it have a more universal significance and to what extent?" A statement may carry a high degree of inspiration and yet be directed only to the current situation in which it is offered. Such judgments concerning the extent of its applications will then be instructive in determining the appropriate stance toward any statement from scripture, or from any other authoritative source.

The following table contains twelve statements, the first two from *Saints Herald* editorials and the remainder from the scriptures of the church. Some may embody beliefs that were prevalent in the society or church at that time, while others might express principles that are more universal. Give an opinion on each of the statements, using the following code:

1 = substantially limited and applicable to the specific historical or cultural setting;

2 = somewhat time-bound, but having some relevance beyond the immediate setting;

3 = stating a universal principle or truth appropriate for all times and situations.

---

1. "The body of Mrs. Ben Pittman...was cremated in Washington, Pennsylvania, Feb. 15, 1878. The story of how the body was subjected to the fiery ordeal and reduced to ashes...horrible, unnatural, and impossible as

---

it may seem, is related in the papers of the day...as an interesting evidence of the hardness of heart, the seeming entire loss of natural affection even in the nearest and dearest associations of life, in these degenerate and ungodly days."—*Saints' Herald* (1878): 71 _____

2. "In this connection we may say that, when womankind leave the sphere assigned them by nature's God and seek to meddle with what, by nature, is reserved for men to do, they excite only the pity and contempt of all sensible people.... Politics does not appertain to woman's place...a mannish woman is a sort of social monstrosity.... Happy are they who recognize and abide submissively by these eternal facts."—*Saints' Herald* (1888): 713 _____

3. "If someone has a stubborn and rebellious son who will not obey his father and mother, who does not heed them when they discipline him...all the men of the town shall stone him to death."—Deuteronomy 21:18, 21 NRSV

4. "Anyone who divorces his wife and marries another commits adultery, and whoever marries a woman divorced from her husband commits adultery." [Jesus to the Pharisees]
—Luke 16:18 NRSV; 16:23 IV _____

5. "Then Peter came and said to him, 'Lord, if another member of the church sins against me, how often should I forgive? As many as seven times?' Jesus said to him, 'Not seven times, but I tell you seventy-seven times.'"
—Matthew 18:21–22 NRSV _____

6. "Verily, thus saith the Lord, I require [of members] all their surplus property to be put into the hands of the bishop of my church of Zion...and this shall be the beginning of the tithing of my people; and after that, those who been thus tithed, shall pay one tenth of all their interest annually; and this shall be a standing law unto them forever...."

—Doctrine and Covenants 106:1 _____

7. "Nevertheless, let the organ and the stringed instrument, and the instrument of brass be silent when the Saints assemble for prayer and testimony, that the feelings of the tender and sad may not be intruded upon."

—Doctrine and Covenants 119:6e _____

8. "Every man praying or prophesying, having his head covered, dishonoreth his head. But every women that prayeth or prophesieth with her head uncovered dishonoreth her head.... For if the woman be not covered, let her also be shorn."—I Corinthians 11:4–6 IV _____

9. "Let your women keep silence in the churches; for it is not permitted unto them to speak [IV, reads "rule"]; but they are commanded to be under obedience, as also saith the law. And if they will learn any thing, let them ask their husbands at home, for it is a shame for women to speak [IV, reads "rule"] in the church."

—I Corinthians 14:34–35 KJV _____

10. "Let the women learn in silence with all subjection. For I suffer not a woman to teach...but to be in silence."—I Timothy 2:11–12 ___

11. "Thou shalt not be proud in thy heart; let all thy garments be plain, and their beauty the beauty of the work of thine own hands."
    —Doctrine and Covenants 42:12a ___

12. "Therefore, do not wonder that some women of the church are being called to priesthood responsibilities. This is in harmony with my will.—Doctrine and Covenants 156:9c

TOTAL ___

Key: 15 or below: You tend to attribute a strong cultural influence to scripture.

16–21: You take a moderate stance with respect to the impact of culture.

22 and above: You tend to attribute a low influence by culture.

4. Discuss any of the items listed above. What is their significance for the positions or understandings that members of the RLDS Church may develop today? Are there some about which individual members are more likely to differ? Why?

Facing Up to Our Biases

It will be necessary to recognize that while we are making judgments about the extent to which cultural influences affect any statement, we who are making these judgments are ourselves creatures of culture. Unless by some means as yet undiscovered we can escape our environment, throwing off the distortions of its biases, we are obliged to deal with life and truth in the presence of those biases. This is by no means the least of the hazards facing the person who approaches theology seriously.

We need to acknowledge the strength of those "prejudices," which act as a series of lenses through which we view the world. We "see through a glass darkly" as we come to our understandings about what is true and what is real. M. Scott Peck believes that the burden of changing our conceptual maps is so difficult and painful that many people have given up by the end of middle age. However, our biases need not hold us in total captivity. Peck believes that human beings also possess the capacity for self-transcendence, the capacity to institute changes that transform who we are and what we "see." It is possible to develop a high cultural awareness, for any person to acknowledge his or her own personal/historical/cultural particularities and yet to a significant degree move beyond the parochialism of space, gender, tribe, age, education, social class, or religious community.

While our particular biases may result in a narrow or distorted vision, and may make it difficult for us to be impartial in our judgments, they may also serve to illuminate. Although the term "bias" is generally used in a negative sense, it is applied here simply to mean "an inclination of temperament or outlook." Thus the bias arising from my age may mean that I find it difficult to adjust to new ideas or to feel in harmony with younger people. But it may also mean that I bring some experience and time-tested perspectives to bear on situations. Again, I believe that my upbringing in the RLDS tradition did expose me to some concepts and attitudes that were less than valid or helpful. But that same tradition has also nurtured me in a network of treasured experiences and values that would be difficult to duplicate elsewhere.

Given the all-encompassing influence of our culture upon us, how can we minimize its negative impact? First, simply to be aware of our biases, to acknowledge the fact that we do view the world through these lenses, is an effective starting point. This calls for the confession that we are indeed flawed and myopic creatures, seeing dimly a minute segment of the world we inhabit. Most of us, for example, have had occasion to perceive how difficult it is for those outside the RLDS tradition to appreciate the essence of our faith as we have experienced it from within. We may have read evaluations or attacks on the church and wondered how the authors could be so prejudiced or narrow-minded. If we can then remember that we must have equal difficulty representing other faiths adequately, we have taken one small step toward dealing with bias.

Second, we can cultivate eyes to see and ears to hear those with different cultural perspectives. At the end of his first day in an Independence elementary school after moving from Australia, our seven-year-old son came home with the startling news that everybody in his class spoke English. Having lived in an environment where many neighborhood and school friends represented several cultures and spoke a variety of languages, the mere exposure to a different environment raised his consciousness of the world about him. The World Conference is but one of many settings where this opportunity exists. The representation of people from other cultures will increase with time, as will the technology to enable non-English speaking delegates to participate equally in dialogue and debate. Not only in this environment, but in others we will need to repress the instinct to assume the superiority of our own insights and perspectives.

Third, we can learn to suspend judgment while engaged in the process, resisting the temptation to come to premature closure. This means that we will maintain a delicate balance between conviction concerning what we believe to be valid and openness to the possibility that there is more to be understood. From time to time, while traveling by air in my assignments, the conversation with a temporary neighbor has led (with some contrivance on my part) to the beliefs of the Reorganized Church of Jesus Christ of Latter Day Saints. I have often felt it necessary to preface my explanations by saying, "as best we understand at the present time." While this may appear to suggest a lack of real testimony, I am convinced that in times past we would often have been well advised to adopt this approach.

Fourth, we can subject our own perceptions to scrutiny. How did they arise? How capable of mature judgment were we when specific beliefs were first accepted? To profess that I learned certain things "at my mother's knee" or from my junior high Sunday school teacher is no guarantee of their validity. Upon what evidence or data were those ideas based? Have I discussed them in settings where they could be tested? Do I feel threatened and defensive when any of those ideas are challenged?

5. The author suggests that there are occasions when it might be preferable to qualify statements of belief with the preface "as best we know at the present time." Evaluate this position. Are there times when it would be appropriate? Not appropriate?

6. In what situations have you had opportunity to test ideas learned in childhood, or when you first became a member of the RLDS Church? Have these situations provided the grounds for you to modify or change any of those beliefs?

Strangers and Pilgrims

Although Christians will of necessity participate as citizens in the larger social setting in which they live, they may sometimes feel out of step, marching to a different drumbeat. Members of the Restoration movement have referred to this as the need to be "in the world but not of it."[6] This is neither to imply withdrawal from the world (as it was sometimes interpreted to mean) or indifference to what happens in our communities and the larger society. Rather, the call to be found "in the forefront"[7] presses the church to consider what understandings and values will guide its participation in the various neighborhoods and cultures in which the church exists.

Some values prominent in the larger society we will appreciate, applaud, and support as they are perceived to be in harmony with the mission of the church. Others, no matter how widely they may be accepted and praised, we may judge to be out of harmony with and even injurious to the cause of the gospel. For instance, in a society that applauds the movers and shakers or the influential and powerful, that respects those who vehemently insist on their individual rights, there may be little place for those who live out the servant mode, or who render themselves vulnerable by compassion. Those who take up the standard of peacemakers may find themselves in the minority in a culture where violence appears to saturate public life. When self-gratification becomes the highest priority for significant segments of the population, self-discipline and restraint will appear quaint. When individualism has a high priority, the nurture of community may rank low on the scale of values. In the view of sociologist Robert Bellah, it is this sense of community that has been tragically lost in American life, after having proved central to the experience of the early colonies.[8]

Anthony Chvala-Smith has produced a resource for the Communities of Joy emphasis that identifies core values for RLDS members.[9] Chvala-Smith lists the following as values that have been highly prized and embodied in the fellowship.

163

Such values inevitably must exert a strong influence on the way the church undertakes its theological exploration. The writer states: "But by looking for patterns of meaning—that is, recurring structures that embody the experience of the movement—we will situate beliefs and doctrines in their proper context. The gospel, in other words, is not only the truth, but the *way* and the *life.*"[10]

The following core values are affirmed:

- *the centrality of Jesus Christ:* a lively sense of the presence and power of Christ in the personal and corporate life of church members;
- *the fellowship of the Saints:* the close sense of belonging that links members and transcends the barriers of culture or geographic distance;
- *the experience of the prophetic Spirit:* the conviction that the Holy Spirit enlivens and prompts the response of individuals and the body at large;
- *the transforming impulse:* a commitment to the regeneration of society (in RLDS language, "the cause of Zion");
- *the expectation of new things:* a sure hope in the future of God; the sense that a marvelous work is *always* about to break forth.

Although these values may be expressed in different terms, they are the underlying convictions, rooted in experience, that link belief to action, that shape our understanding of the mission of the church, that provide the priorities for the life of the congregation. It is these themes that most RLDS members would describe, in one way or another, if called on to explain why they give their allegiance to a small denomination that expects a great deal of its people, and offers only the demanding path of discipleship.

There is no need to "prove" or justify these values: they are too deeply rooted and confirmed in the life of the church to call for proof or justification. If any one of them should be ignored or distorted, the outcome would very quickly be noticeable in the impoverishment of the church's worship and witness. It is these values that, no matter how they might be described or categorized, hold theology to account and empower the church to enter faithfully into the life of the surrounding culture even while maintaining its stance as "strangers and pilgrims":

> Christian faith calls people to freedom and responsibility in every sphere of life. Thus an indispensable task of theology is to ask how the gospel might reform and transform human life in concrete ways in our own time and in our own situation.... What patterns of our own life, what institutional structures that we may have long taken for granted, must now be called in question by the gospel? What structures of evil must be named and challenged if the gospel is to have any concrete impact on human life in the present?[11]

---

7. Identify the various ways the phrase "in the world but not of it" may be understood. What do you think it means for the church, or for you personally?
8. Discuss the core values listed by Anthony Chvala-Smith as basic to the life of the church. How do you experience these in your congregation? Are there other values that you would consider sufficiently influential to be placed alongside these?

The purpose of this chapter has been to support the position that all communication, including inspired communication, is influenced by the cultural environment in which the writers or speakers find themselves. One conclusion that could possibly be drawn from this discussion is that scripture is thereby discredited and untrustworthy.

This has certainly not been my conclusion. The RLDS Church has invested and continues to invest great respect and trust in the scriptures. But to say that we trust the "word of God" is not to commit ourselves to a literal and universally applicable interpretation of every view reflected therein. It is rather to affirm that we can trust the God who has spoken through other imperfect witnesses to be actively present in our own lives. The same Spirit that illuminated the minds and understandings of our predecessors enables us to discern the meaning of the gospel in the concrete situations of our contemporary lives.

Activities for the Reader

A. List some of the prevailing values that you perceive in the cultural environment that surrounds you.

B. Identify those values you consider to be positive and in harmony with the principles of the gospel. If possible, cite one scriptural reference, or World Conference resolution that supports your opinion.

C. Identify those that you consider to be in conflict with gospel values. If possible, cite one scriptural reference or World Conference resolution to support your opinion.

Notes

1. Joseph Smith III, "Pleasant Chats" in *The True Latter Day Saints' Herald* 1, no. 4 (February 15, 1869): 115.
2. *Webster's New Collegiate Dictionary*, 1981 edition.
3. Walter N. Johnson, "Inspiration, Generation, Transmission, and Reception," *University Bulletin* 12, no. 1 (Fall 1959): 59.
4. Roy A. Cheville, *Scriptures from Ancient America: A Study of the Book of Mormon* (Independence, Missouri: Herald House, 1964), 136.
5. Roy A. Cheville, *The Book of Mormon Speaks for Itself* (Independence, Missouri: Herald House, 1971), 23.
6. Doctrine and Covenants 128:8b.
7. Doctrine and Covenants 150:7, 151:9.
8. Robert Bellah, et al., *Habits of the Heart: Individualism and Commitment in American Life* (Berkeley, California: University of California Press, 1986).
9. Anthony Chvala-Smith, *Core Values of the RLDS Church* in the *Congregational Leaders Handbook*, Communities of Joy, B-1 (Independence, Missouri: Herald House, 1994).
10. Ibid., 2.
11. Daniel L. Migliori, *Faith Seeking Understanding: An Introduction to Christian Theology* (Grand Rapids, Michigan: William B. Eerdmans, 1991), 13.

Chapter 11

Is Creative Dissent Possible?

"In the first century, amidst a plethora of fresh dissent, the sober counsel was 'Test everything; hold fast what is good.' It is sober counsel for every century, and every generation. Dissent neither conducts the examination nor controls the results: it only ensures throughout history that testing will take place."

—Edwin Scott Gaustad, *Dissent in American Religion*

"But, stop, Mr. Editor, do you really mean to say that Saints quarrel in meeting? Yes; we mean to say that exactly; or perhaps we ought to qualify it thus: those who have been baptized, and have made a profession of faith, do quarrel in meeting; and that too, over the administration of Church affairs. It is a very unsatisfactory thing to say, or write; but as it exists, and to the no small discredit of the church in the place and region where it occurs, we feel to write of it."

—Editorial, *Saints' Herald* (1879): 168

The concept and practice of dissent has enjoyed a long and, for the most part, honorable tradition. When dissenters within the Church of England pressed for reform in the sixteenth century, Elizabeth I, titular head of the church, was not supportive. Her successor, James I, was even less sympathetic, threatening to "harry them out of the land, or else do worse." While most of these aspiring reformers (nonseparatist Puritans) stayed within the ranks, a significant number "separated" and sought to establish their own covenant. Some were indeed harried out of England, and found refuge in the Low Countries, where nonconformists were allowed freedom to practice their religion.

While the Puritans in Virginia were content with the Church of England, which had been established as the official faith in that colony, others who came to the New World brought their strong dissenting stance with them. It was from Leiden that John Robinson led a group of dissenters to New England and established a colony at Plymouth. Here and in other settlements, notably at Massachusetts Bay, the Puritan movement, born in England, would find its greatest expression. It is intriguing to note that the Puritans, founded in dissent, reached no ready agreement among themselves as to the precise form their religion should take:

> Puritans argued...that Christians should do only what the Bible commanded. Unfortunately for the Puritans, when they came to power in England, and to a lesser extent when some had migrated to America, they could never agree among themselves exactly what scripture mandated for a wide variety of practical matters, including the basic question of church government—whether a reformed episcopacy, congregationalism, presbyterianism, or even liberty of conscience.[1]

The Puritan dissenters found it difficult to tolerate dissent within their own ranks. Their strong insistence on the foundational principle of the covenanted community made it difficult to accept pluralism, either in England or the American settlements. In the course of time true Puritans were encountering dissent from such as Anne Hutchinson and Roger Williams, who shared the spiritual heritage of Puritanism, and also from Baptists, themselves offshoots of English Puritanism. The first Quakers met instant opposition in Puritan strongholds. Matthew Fox was fiercely opposed by Roger Williams during his visit to the colonies, and several Quakers were hanged for their religious faith. Mennonites, Dutch Reformed, and Swedish Lutherans were also threatening the Puritan vision of an undivided divine commonwealth for the New Jerusalem.

Although pluralism was an established fact by the time of the revolution, persecution of Catholics, Jews, Presbyterians, Quakers (who opposed the slave trade), Mennonites, and Presbyterians persisted. With the gradual disappearance of the state-established and supported church (Connecticut in 1818 and Massachusetts in 1833 were the last) toleration became the widely recognized principle. Groups would still experience persecution from time to time—the experience of the Saints being a case in point—but the most lively dissent, and the reactions provoked by it, would occur *within* religious communities. Freedom of religion, and the emphasis on personal conscience, has virtually guaranteed diversity of belief, expressed with varying degrees of intensity. Over time, as might safely be anticipated, movements have experienced fragmentation as adherents have followed their conscience in different directions.

1. Do you find any parallel in Reorganization history to the difficulty of achieving agreement among the Puritans? To what extent may this be attributed to the emphasis on the united community expressed by both groups?
2. The author expresses the opinion that dissent and fragmentation are virtually assured by the profession of freedom of religion and personal conscience. Do you think this is an overstatement? Give reasons for your point of view.

Dissent among the Elect

Although the Restoration movement itself began as a dissenting body, the Saints have continued to experience dissent almost from the first few months of the organization of the church in 1830. Steven Shields's book *Divergent Paths of the Restoration*[2] documents the rise and course of many of these fragmenting movements. It should come as no surprise that each of the three editions following its initial appearance have been "revised and enlarged." With the passage of time it is to be expected that such groups will continue to increase in number.

As is more generally the case, some have been proud to bear the title of "dissenter." Others have objected, especially if the term was understood to convey "unfaithful." Dissenters have invariably insisted on their faithfulness, and the apostasy or heresy of those from whom they have chosen to stand apart. Whatever the case, it would appear that freedom of religion as we know and experience it is the sure guarantor of dissent. This is not because people are casual about their beliefs, but rather because they are deeply committed to them. In this connection it is important to distinguish between complaint and dissent: the first signifies some measure of dissatisfaction with matters great or small; the second refers to deeply felt resistance to fundamental issues.

In the course of Christian history, antagonists have charged opponents with a wide variety of defects: absence of the Holy Spirit; weakness in the faith; misinterpretation of the scriptures; errors in orientation (liberal, fundamental, secularist, etc.); disloyalty to tradition or to precedent; personal ambition or priorities; and faulty reasoning. These have invariably been the accusations accompanying the discussion of major differences among the Saints.

Many years ago the story was told of a professor of children's education at the University of Sydney who had just finished having his driveway surfaced when some neighborhood children ran across the new concrete, leaving the imprint of their shoes on the surface. This provoked the intense ire of the professor. His next-door neighbor intervened to say: "But

Doctor _____, everybody knows how you just love children." To this he replied: "In the abstract, madam, but not in the concrete."

This goes to the heart of the issue of pluralism. In theory, the principle might be readily praiseworthy, but it will be severely tested in the concrete situations that arise in congregations, and in the wider assemblies of the membership:

> [T]he Reorganized Church was born from the same dissenting tradition that is one of the hallmarks of the Latter Day Saint movement. Throughout its history, the Reorganized Church has struggled with issues of pluralism, attempting to provide the delicate balance of a middle ground. But, as history illustrates, this is a precariously difficult position to maintain.[3]

Because of the particular circumstances in which the Reorganization emerged, congregational freedom and diversity were probably at their highest during the 1850s, described by Roger Launius as "the golden age of Reorganization autonomy." To a considerable degree the trend toward centralized government characterizing the later years of Joseph Smith Jr. was relaxed among the scattered remnants who eventually came into the Reorganization. In the intervening years many of these members had maintained their connection through isolated congregational ties. Even after the initial organizing phases of 1853, members maintained a strong measure of congregational autonomy, essentially adopting a waiting stance in uncertain anticipation of what the future would bring. This tendency toward localism was neither automatically nor readily abandoned by the coming together of these various strands:

> There had always been a dynamic present in Mormonism creating an impetus toward a strong hierarchical structure versus the tradition of a strong congregational structure.... The Reorganized Church... developed its personality out of the themes of dissent and American pluralism. The people of the Reorganized Church represented that strain of early Mormonism that was less extreme, more tolerant, and undeniably and incessantly democratic in its outlook. The early Re-

171

organization embraced and celebrated those trends. A diversity of congregations, a diversity of personalities, a diversity of ideas all came together in only the loosest of organizations before the ordination of Joseph Smith III to the presidency.[4]

The perceived need for a greater coordination of the several parts, for some focused direction for program and objectives, and for greater efficiency in managing the resources of personnel and finances would move such a loose confederation in the direction of centralized supervision. This was indeed not out of harmony with the expectations of the Saints, who had anticipated, and then welcomed, the coming of Joseph III, and looked to him for prophetic direction. These needs, reasonable within themselves, and the impact of the dissenting activity of significant figures, such as the apostles Henry Deam, and later Jason W. Briggs and Zenos H. Gurley Jr., provided the motivation for the increasing centralization of authority in the hands of the hierarchy. Aware of the unfortunate impact of fragmentation after 1844 and in responding to dissenting pressures, the first president of the Reorganization acted from this conviction:

> [I]f the Reorganized Church was to accomplish anything of worth it had to unify and focus its efforts along a concentrated path. To do so required enough centralized direction that the system functioned with a degree of efficiency. Tolerance and sympathy could be accepted, even demanded, but when it significantly impinged on the accomplishment of church objectives then it had to be curtailed.[5]

Dissent in the Reorganization has been virtually continuous, spirited, and frequently divisive. With the passage of time, the perceived need to preserve and defend the "Old Jerusalem Gospel" gave a sharpened edge to divergence of opinion. This has been particularly true to the extent that the "gospel" has been understood as a set or system of specific dogmas, communicated by direct revelation and sealed by tradition, distinct from and superior to all other understandings of the Christian message. Under these circumstances any perceived departure or development is, by definition, apostasy. Although the Reorganization has long affirmed its noncreedal stance, and even though such tenets as are "necessary to obedience and salvation" (GCR 222) have never been clearly articulated or officially acted upon, dissent has often sprung from the conviction that these tenets were engraved in stone.

Although Joseph Smith III had frequently upheld the principle of freedom of conscience, and had denied the existence (most notably at the General Conference of 1910, as noted earlier) of any ultimate judge of orthodoxy of belief in the church, this open stance was frequently difficult to maintain in practice. The First Presidency, acting as *Herald* editors and often under the heading of "Pleasant Chats," tended to reflect hardened views from time to time on matters of faith, as if these had the status of official dogma. In debating the matter of doctrine with Utah Mormons, the president insisted that a traditional belief of the church was "that when a principle of the...gospel was once fixed by revelation, it was thenceforward to be as a 'nail driven in a sure place,' upon which the Saints and the world could rely as unchangeable and unmovable by men or devils."[6]

---

3. Discuss the difficulty of attempting to maintain a balance between unity and pluralism at the various levels of church life. What tenets, if any, should be established as firmly as a "nail driven in a sure place?"

It is of interest to note that Joseph, undertaking to adopt the same firm position on the matter of the virgin birth, confused that concept with one substantially different—the doctrine of the Immaculate Conception—which had received the status of dogma for Roman Catholics following its teaching by Pope Pius IX in 1854:

We learn with regret that there is now and then an elder who believes and teaches, against the doctrine of the immaculate conception of Christ....

To hold that the scriptural relation of the immaculate conception of Jesus is untrue is to accept him as less than Christ. We can have no confidence for our salvation in one simply mortal in his conception and life.... The fact of his immaculate conception is necessary to the validity of his claim as the Son of God, and this claim is essential to the existence and truthfulness of the plan of salvation.[7]

The prophet's fear was that dissenting views could threaten the unity of the faith, and perhaps eventually impugn the revelations of Joseph Smith Jr. and the divinity of the Book of Mormon. Smith found it difficult to regard the holders of such questions, regardless of their credentials, as anything but "discontented disbelievers." His conclusion appears to invest confidence in the majority view as holding authority:

If the church could consistently yield one well accredited and commonly received teaching, or tenet, of which the majority were satisfied as to its validity, there could be none, not one, which they might not be called on to give up. It would be but a question of time as to when the church would be indeed not only without a creed but without a faith.[8]

The inconsistency between principle and practice was evident in such matters as the debate over the nature of the Godhead. Israel Smith stated some years later that the matter of the Godhead was "one among possibly hundreds of theological questions wherein one will not become a heretic however wrong he may be." His father, however, insisted that the tradition of the elders in the matter should be accorded respect. Despite the vagueness of the notion of personages of spirit and of tabernacle, and the fragility of the evidence on which it rested, Joseph believed this binding on the church:

It is a long accredited belief of the Church that the Godhead is not a unit, but that there are two *personages*, the Father and the Son.... If, upon some other points the principles were as practically, clearly stated in the formulas of the belief of the Church as the number of personages in the Godhead, there are some brethern [sic] who would not now be looked upon as half-way heretics.[9]

In similar fashion the president thought it necessary to resist the encroachment of the view that interpreted some of the historical accounts and characters of Genesis as *myth*, in the religious sense of the word, even though the question was manifestly not one "necessary for salvation." While to some Adam might be a symbol, Joseph wrote: "To us, [he] is a reality, an entity, a being like ourselves; save only, that being created in the image of God he was in physical development the best type of what man should be."[10]

The foregoing illustrates the difficulty of walking the narrow line between conviction and openness, between unity of faith and pluralism, even from one like Joseph III, clearly moderate in disposition and anxious for the preservation of mutual respect in the midst of diversity. Others less kindly disposed, and unburdened by the need to keep an eye to the health of the institution, would be notably more intense, even hostile, in their defense of the "faith."

> 4. Discuss the importance of establishing some firm declaration about the Godhead (the nature of and relationship between God, Christ, and the Holy Spirit). Do you have a clearly developed personal view in this matter? What do you think the majority of church members would believe? Have you heard the issue discussed recently?

175

5. Joseph Smith III was concerned that unless there was some standardization of belief the time might come when the church could not only be without a creed, but without a faith. To what extent, if at all, has this happened in the Reorganization? What evidence can you cite to support your opinion? Do you see an inconsistency on the president's part in supporting freedom of opinion and yet taking such a strong stand on certain issues?

A Place for Heresy?

The notion of heresy, or in more familiar terms, apostasy, figures prominently in the history of the Restoration. Understood as the promotion of an opinion or doctrine contrary to the truth or to generally accepted belief, the charge of heresy may be leveled in two directions, either toward members of the organization by those in authority or by dissenting members toward those in authority. It appears that in the Utah Mormon tradition the charge has most often been directed toward "apostate" members. In more recent years at least, it has been leaders in the Reorganization who have more frequently come under this indictment. Because of the hesitation of those leaders to take dogmatic stands against members, formal charges of apostasy, or heresy, have rarely been invoked.

Charges of heresy are most difficult to prove in those bodies that have no clearly defined creedal statement. Moreover, "heretics" have made their own contribution to the clarifying of Christian faith, as suggested by Timothy F. Lull:

Is heresy possible? Certainly. At least I hope so. A church that cannot experience heresy probably doesn't have any commitments, any identity, any character. The possibility of heresy is simply the negative expression of a church's having a confession of faith.... Is heresy possible? Unfortunately. I say this because the defining and

176

maintaining of the boundaries of the community is one of the church's most delicate tasks, and one that can easily be handled in a way that brings shame or even scorn on the church itself. It calls for deeper wisdom and greater political skill than the human situation is generally able to muster.[11]

The apostle Paul was concerned about the divisiveness of false teaching and repeatedly pleaded for unity in the Corinthian church. The same concern led him to remind the congregation at Philippi, and specific members within it, of the virtues of peace and unity: "Make my joy complete: be of the same mind, having the same love, being in full accord and of one mind.... I urge Euodia and I urge Syntyche to be of the same mind in the Lord.[12]

On the other hand, as many scholars have pointed out, there were "heretics" in the early church, gifted intellectually and spiritually, who made significant contributions to the development of the faith. Such a one was Marcion, whose efforts to establish a selection of writings compatible with his own beliefs awakened the church to the need to identify an authorized canon as the norm for faith and belief:

> The history of heresy illustrates the worn adage that the church did not know what it believed until someone stated its teaching partially or wrongly. Christian doctrine did not come into the world fully formed but was formulated as the result of controversy and debate, of correction and patient refinement of terms, phrases, and concepts over generations and centuries. Often the "heretics" were the first to sense the limitations of traditional formulations, to pose fresh questions, or to retrieve biblical texts and themes that had been forgotten or ignored.[13]

---

6. Can you identify beliefs or positions that could have been considered heretical when first advocated, but that have become accepted parts of the faith and practice of the church? How did these ideas gain acceptance?

---

7. Do you see a place for the "heretic" in the church today? Given the undefined nature of the Reorganization's beliefs, how would a heretic be identified? Should there be limits on what such a person could advocate, or the manner of his or her advocacy of ideas?

The Dissenter's Dilemma

The statement titled "The Ethics of Dissent" issued by the Standing High Council in 1988 expressed the desire to "affirm the value of dissent in the consensus process of the church." At its theoretical best, the practice of dissent enriches the life of the church by providing an open forum for the examination of doctrines and practices maintained by tradition, or by opening to scrutiny new possibilities implicit in the gospel:

> First, in its purest form religious dissent becomes necessary when the individual believes the integrity of the gospel and the self are at stake. To dissent is not merely to hold certain beliefs, but involves the decision to confess those beliefs publicly against the beliefs of others because one comes to believe that the essential core of the gospel is at stake. Dissent, then, in its purest form, is a centered act of faith, necessitated and demanded by the integrity of the gospel and the self, but undertaken for the good of the whole community.[14]

Dissent may be expressed about peripheral or minor matters, but the differences need not be divisive, even hardly worthy of the term. But the very gravity of the questions over which dissent may arise creates a dilemma. For the member outside the higher levels of authority there may well be a sense of urgency, and even of calling. These feelings may exist alongside the feeling of powerlessness, of the difficulty of gaining access to the attention of those in authority. The legislative arenas of the church, particularly those beyond the local level, may not be the most favorable environments for free and careful perusal of significant matters. The mechanics of the rules of order seldom engender theological exploration, but tend to thrust those who want to begin the process into adversarial positions.

Equally, church employees, or those holding positions of considerable status and authority, may experience a dilemma of a different kind. How does such a person express dissent of significant dimension without being open to the charge of disloyalty, or of disrupting the leadership's image of unity? To accept a call to authoritative ministry in the Reorganization is tacitly to approve doctrines and practices established by tradition and approved by the body. To raise not trifling but serious questions about some aspects of the "contract" to which such a person has agreed may readily be judged an act of disloyalty, and this may be seen by those outside the institution as revealing cracks in the foundation of the movement. This is the dilemma that Paul Edwards describes:

> To loyal members it would appear that dissent is disloyal, disloyal to the movement that existed when we made a contract. Thus it is unethical for us to attempt to change the contract made with the General Will, for such a change violates the promise made as prescriptions of the past extend to the present and the future.[15]

Nevertheless, unless the Reorganization is understood as a closed and finalized system of prescriptive positions then it may well be expected that dissent will continue to characterize its life. Unless principles are established and honored for such a future, the historical pattern will persist: Each new venture into the unknown will yield its customary loss of members, so that the course of the movement becomes a cycle of admitting new members through the front door while others leave through the back door, as it were. Taking a point of departure from our present experience, Larry Conrad has written:

> The best approach for all sides in this time of reformation and dissent would be to look once again at the stories of the tradition and to

reread the stories of the Christian faith. The texts of the faith have stories to tell which could bring a saving message. The value of dissent is that it can contribute to a fresh, more responsible hearing of the stories and to a more faithful interpretation of the Christian tradition in the context of the Reorganization.[16]

---

8. If prospective members of the church are introduced to a community that is still in the developmental stage, with the possibility of changes in the future, what kind of security can be offered? Is it preferable for new members to discover this aspect of the Reorganization at the outset rather than being faced with it when some new possibility appears on the horizon?

Principles for Dissent

If dissent is to be practiced under the most favorable conditions, without such barriers or constraints as may eventually provoke contention, what principles should guide the process? As indicated earlier in this chapter, the Standing High Council issued a statement in 1988 undertaking to set out such principles.[17] After tracing the history of dissent in the movement, both through the original church and the Reorganization, the council listed the following as criteria for the ethical expression of dissent:

1. the responsibility of all members to work peacefully, yet assertively, for appropriate resolution of issues in a spirit of reconciliation;

2. the willingness to assent or dissent on specific issues as members deem appropriate;

3. the readiness to listen to alternative views with an open mind and objectively consider accurately documented evidence, and to prepare well-documented statements should the issue be considered unsatisfactorily resolved;

4. the willingness to make dissenting statements in the appropriate arenas, such as legislative sessions, administrative meetings, or personal situations;

5. the willingness to study the issues and attend authorized discussions and business sessions, addressing issues rather than impugning the character of those holding opposing positions;

6. the freedom for church employees to hold different opinions and express dissent in the proper arenas of the work place;

7. the willingness of those in leadership positions to observe both the spirit and the letter of the law in the presiding role; and

8. the right to withdraw from activities considered destructive to one's faith and relationship to God, but not to withhold or encourage others to withhold tithing or general funds with a view to thwarting programs authorized by the World Conference.

How to cultivate the environment in which these principles can be observed, and to what extent they can enable members to address critical issues, must be a matter for judgment and for future experience. The council's principles included the statement that "it is never ethical to persuade people to act contrary to a divine commandment." This appears to overlook the fact that virtually all dissent arises from opinions as to whether certain commandments, prescriptions, laws, or procedures are indeed divine in their origin. The ordination of women, baptism for the dead, open Communion, the relation of the RLDS Church to other churches, or the conditions of membership are but representative of the category of questions that might provoke dissent. In fact, it is difficult to conceive of dissent that *does not* arise from differing convictions about whether the matters in contention are of divine origin. What to one person may be a "divine commandment" may to another be nothing more than human contrivance, even reversing something of divine origin.

The constructive expression of dissent is at the same time a high priority for the church's theological discipline, and a stark illustration of the hazardous nature of the undertaking. In view of the varying degrees of effectiveness in creating and even encouraging the fruitful climate for dissent, it may well prove to be one of the major challenges facing the denomination in the years to come. From an informed nonmember's point of view:

> The most pressing theological need in the church is to articulate a compelling, comprehensive theological vision that creatively and faithfully integrates Reorganization symbols and stories with the wider Christian tradition in the modern context. To discern this vision *all* voices, including dissenting voices, must be heard.[18]

---

9. Discuss the principles stated by the Standing High Council and evaluate how they may be applied in specific situations. Discuss the difficulties that arise when any one of these principles is ignored.
10. The council stated that when a decision is made in a legislative setting following free expression of opinion, mutual respect and prayer, "those who were not on the prevailing side must accept it in faith, [because] there is no other way to accept it." Evaluate the degree to which this guideline has been effective in specific situations.

Activities for the Reader

A. Write down what you consider to be the three most important principles or procedures to observe in a situation of dissent. Write a brief statement specifying what each principle requires of the dissenting parties.
B. Imagine that a decision has been reached by a majority that strongly offends your sense of rightness or faithfulness. Perhaps such a decision has already been implemented in the life of the church. State in writing what the options fac-

ing you would be, and how you would respond to this situation.

Notes

1. *Eerdmans' Handbook of Christianity in America* (Grand Rapids, Michigan: William P. Eerdmans, 1983), 22.
2. Steven L. Shields, *Divergent Paths of the Restoration: A History of the Latter Day Saint Movement*, Fourth Edition, Revised and Enlarged (Los Angeles, California: Restoration Research, 1990).
3. Steven L. Shields, "An Overview of Dissent in the Reorganization" in Roger D. Launius and W. B. "Pat" Spillman, eds., *Let Contention Cease* (Independence, Missouri: Graceland/Park Press, 1991), 62. The essays in this volume constitute the most helpful gathering of views on dissent in the Reorganization currently available under one cover.
4. Roger D. Launius, "Guarding Prerogatives: Autonomy and Dissent in the Development of the Nineteenth-Century Reorganized Church" in *Let Contention Cease*, 27, 36.
5. Ibid., 47.
6. *The True Latter Day Saints' Herald* 24, no. 3 (February 1, 1877): 40.
7. Ibid., 17, no. 11 (January 1, 1870): 336.
8. Ibid., 33, no. 19 (May 15, 1886): 289.
9. Ibid., 24, no. 3 (February 1, 1877): 42.
10. Ibid., 18, no. 23 (December 1, 1871): 720.
11. Timothy F. Lull, "Is Heresy Possible? Yes, Unfortunately" in *Word & World* VIII, no. 2: 109.
12. Philippians 2:2, 4:2 (NRSV).
13. Robert W. Wilken, "The Durability of Orthodoxy," in *Word & World,* VIII, no. 20: 125–26.
14. Larry W. Conrad, "Dissent Among Dissenters: Theological Dimensions of Dissent in the Reorganization," in *Let Contention Cease*, 203.
15. Paul M. Edwards, "Ethics and Dissent in Mormonism: A Personal Essay," in *Let Contention Cease*, 254.
16. Larry W. Conrad, 229.
17. Standing High Council, "The Ethics of Dissent," *Saints Herald* 145, no. 2 (April 1988): 141–146.
18. Larry W. Conrad, 231.

Chapter 12

Moving into the Future

"So, ever and always, the living spirit of God is the guide and mentor of the theologian, who recognizes that any present formulation of his faith is not irrevocable, but such formulation needs constantly to be illumined and interpreted by the Spirit."

— Arthur A. Oakman, "Theology, Its Place and Meaning," *Saints' Herald* 113, no. 9 (May 1, 1966): 25

We limit not the truth of God to our poor reach of mind
By notions of our day and sect, crude, partial, and
    confined.
No, let a new and better hope within our hearts be
    stirred—
The Lord hath yet more light and truth to break forth
    from his word.

— Text by George Rawson (1807–1889)
Hymns of the Saints, No. 309

In the introduction to the 1987 edition of *Exploring the Faith*, Alan Tyree wrote: "We pray that the day will not be long coming when spiritual maturity, faithful pursuit, and scholarly inquiry will result in a new statement of our faith explorations by another generation." This expectation is consistent with the long-held stance of the church with respect to its understanding of the faith. It is also in harmony with the position adopted by the Committee on Basic Beliefs, responsible for the first edition of the book in 1970:

> Such a work is never finished because each generation brings its own unique insights and experience to the task. Of necessity there is a continuity in the history of religious experience so that any generation cannot regard itself as standing alone without meaningful relationship to the past and to the future. On the one hand [they] stand on the shoulders of giants, and on the other they hold in their lives potentially a contribution to the enrichment of the succeeding generations. It is in the tension between what has been and what can be that lives are lived, beliefs tested, and the meaningfulness of contributions is determined.[1]

It has been my objective in this book to enable readers to make a critical examination of the theological task and of the hazards that accompany its successful discharge. We live in an age when such an exploration is seen as hardly relevant, when feelings take priority in determining one's response to and engagement with life, when personal rights are the priority consideration, when sound or thought "bytes" engage the mind and attention for brief instants of time, and when appearance takes priority over essence. Theological "head-trips" inserted into busy schedules and episodic Sunday religious exposures hardly seem worthwhile and sometimes even seem improper.

Nevertheless the times, for members of the Reorganization, are portentous. On the one hand dissenters, following the dictates of conscience and disturbed by the apparent falling away from truth on the part of leaders and policy-makers, organize replicas of the Reorganization structure. Others organize in independent congregations, waiting in expectation of some divine intervention to call a true prophet who can restore order to the movement. Others simply drop out and become inactive. On the other hand church leaders, often at the request of the membership, are confronting serious issues and requesting members to share in careful reflection on these issues. Whether we wish to or not, we are all invited to think and act theologically in a significant time for the church, and probably in a more disciplined manner than at any other time in its history.

Howard Booth has observed that the purpose of theology is not only to describe our human experience but also to explain it. Although this appears a formidable undertaking, it is a process to which every person can contribute something of value. As Howard Booth says:

> Theological systems are ways of explaining the significance and meaning of life's experiences. Differences in theology do not require the denial of anyone's experience; rather, differences reflect only the wide range of specific explanations that are satisfactory to each theologian [author's note: for "theologian" read "person"]. Joseph Smith's religious experiences need not be called into question, for example, but it is clearly legitimate to critique his and others' explanations of them.[2]

1. The First Presidency stated that each generation makes its contribution to the ongoing theological task. What contribution(s) do you think this generation has made to the task since 1970, when this statement appeared in *Exploring the Faith*?
2. Howard Booth said that theology involves not only the criticism of our various experiences, but the critiquing of our explanations of those experiences. Why should each person's explanation of his or her experiences not be sufficient? Why would we wish to critique another's experience, including that of Joseph Smith?

And so members of the Reorganization are encouraged to take responsibility for their theology and to take an active part in shaping our understanding. While some may be assigned to task forces or committees to accept roles in preparing data and recommendations, all share the responsibility for forging the contours of our faith. It is a task that cannot ultimately, or even safely, be delegated to somebody else.

I have also attempted to spell out some of the hazards of the process, likening it to the attempt to negotiate a mine field. However, just as there are detectors to give warning of dangerous ground, so there are principles that can equip the Saints to be more responsible, and more amply rewarded, in their theological dialogue.

In part the hazards have to do with the particular character of the inquiry. While there are resources, such as the scriptures and the testimonies of fellow-searchers, we deal in the final analysis with a mystery. It is not so much that we can commit the object of our inquiries to methodical scrutiny and grasp it. Rather, the essence of our faith is that the Subject of our lives takes hold of and claims us to respond in the spirit of faithful commitment. Even when we feel supremely confident that our experience, our study, and our prayer have opened us to the truth, we can rarely, if ever, feel that our expression of that truth is free of blemish.

Equally hazardous is the character of those undertaking the search. Neither our intelligence, motivations, nor wills are ultimately trustworthy. Many of the early reformers, having rejected the authority of dogma and tradition in favor of trust in the Holy Spirit and scripture, were dismayed to find that contention, differences, and divisiveness persisted. Centuries later Latter Day Saints wonder why it is that individuals of apparently sincere intent—all claiming the guidance of the Spirit and fidelity to the Three Standard Books—can reach such divergent opinions. The fact is, that even given the best of instruments, the researchers are flawed. Indeed, one way of understanding apostasy may be in terms of the continuing tendency of human beings to absolutize the contingent.

Nevertheless, the theological task confronts us with both an urgency and a priority that begs all of our rationalizations. The Reorganization is committed to the search, as painful and beset with uncertainty as it might be, and must be so committed if the call of continuing revelation is taken seriously. Deam Ferris's fine poem is surely in harmony with the sentiments of the hymn text cited at the beginning of this chapter. Members of the Reorganization have felt a kinship with both:

Fountain of all revelation, grant us thy life-giving power;
Without thee no sure salvation, will deliver us this hour.
May no veil of our tradition mask the light that comes from
thee!
Let not pride nor low ambition waste the strength that sets
us free.

We will order not thy wisdom to some cherished form or
mold,
But will search for truths now hidden as we live by those
we hold.

> 3. Discuss Deam Ferris's hymn text. What warnings does it offer those engaged in the theological task? How may those suggestions be implemented?

The Winds of Change

When the First Presidency's article "The Nature of New Revelation" appeared in the *Saints Herald* of February 1984, some readers considered the statement to posit an unreliable or self-contradicting God. The First Presidency appeared, in the eyes of some, to be preparing the way for the denial of a principle written eternally into the nature of the creation and of the gospel, especially when applied to the specific situation that followed closely at the 1984 World Conference. The central point of the statement is universally applicable:

Disjunctive with the past, new revelation brings new insights to the church and points us in new directions. If we really believe in divine revelation, there will always be those moments when the encouragement of the spirit of God in our experience opens up whole new vistas of understanding of his intent and his will for us as his people. We should not only realize that this may occur from time to time, but we should look forward with expectation to those occasions when God will open the windows of heaven and reveal the divine will beyond that which we have previously understood.[3]

Although the term "disjunctive revelation" came to be used in a negative, critical sense by those who saw change as evidence of decay, we see that disjunction, or apparent contradiction, is in the eye of the beholder. Such discontinuity, as the First Presidency stated, is certainly in harmony with our tradition. The Committee on Basic Beliefs had stated earlier, with the publication of *Exploring the Faith*:

> Ours is not a defense of some frozen form but a commitment to life.... This gives to the church flexibility to adjust herself to the call of God in the ever changing world. The church must pay the price to be prophetic by entering the struggle for understanding and interpreting God's will in the midst of every generation.[4]

As suggested in chapter 10, Joseph Smith himself had recognized and responded to this principle, showing a readiness to modify or change the text of the scripture as subsequent experience suggested a more faithful rendition, or changing his mind in the face of further experience, as in the case of the vision concerning his brother Alvin. If the Lord is indeed to bring forth more "light and truth," then surely it must involve more than the crossing of the theological "t's" and the dotting of the theological "i's."

Several months after the World Conference authorized the ordination of women, an article titled "To Be God Is to Appear Changeable" appeared in the *Saints Herald*. As disconcerting as this statement may appear at first sight, the key word "appear," is instructive. Paul Edwards argues that a loving God is not rigid nor inflexible, but rather consistently dependable and trustworthy:

In the main we agree that God does not change in his basic (ultimate) nature. He does not change in his concern, in his love for us, in his willingness to be involved in our lives. On the other hand, we do change. And as a result, because of God's ever reaching concern, there must be a difference—a change—in his approach to us. This enables God to accomplish what was previously impossible because of situations imposed by our agency on his desires.... The question of change arises from our concern for a God who is permanent, truthful, eternal, and everlasting. Our experience is that God as we understand him is constantly in the process of reaching us where we are, and that the prime character of his revealed word affirms his openness to our present needs—not just to our past experiences.[5]

The question of the ordination of women presents a fitting illustration, both of the appropriateness of "disjunctive revelation" and of the nature of a God who may appear changeable to finite human beings. Women had been granted the right to vote at church conferences in 1868, though not without charges that God was unchangeable, and would not endorse a procedure that was new to the life of the church. However, with respect to the ordination of women, Joseph Smith III was adamant. Although women might prophesy or speak in tongues, subject to the judgment of the elders, such freedom did not extend to leading the services or administering the affairs of the congregation. "We do not believe," he wrote in 1876, "that God will so far disregard the rule He himself gives...as to direct important ministerial movements through women or lay members. 'Every man in his place,' means every woman in her place likewise."[6] When earlier addressing the matter, he stated:

All the prophets and apostles that understood the organization of the priesthood, would have looked with astonishment at this new doctrine advocated by some.... Paul, viewing matters in a reasonable way, and beautifully, sets it forth in language like this, "It is a shame for a woman to speak in the church."[7]

A few years later, in 1888, a *Saints' Herald* editorial on the subject of female politicians (a matter very much in the public consciousness) emphatically stated that women had no part in politics, that a woman aspiring to such was "a sort of social monstrosity" who would excite "only the pity and contempt of all sensible people." Advising the Saints that women should not meddle in political affairs, just as men should not interfere with the domestic duties that "pertain alone to women," the editorial concluded that this difference is determinate and unchangeable, and happy are they who recognize and abide submissively by these eternal facts.[8]

It may be of interest to note that anyone supporting the right of women to ordination at that time would have been judged unethical because they were seen as persuading others to deny a "divine commandment." This suggests that "heresy" is as much a matter of timing as it is of substance.

There is no way of knowing how church leaders of the nineteenth century might have responded to the passage of the constitutional amendment granting the franchise to women. Perhaps the passage of time would have led them to recognize that what they had considered as a God-given, "eternal fact" was indeed a manifestation of the limited understanding of human beings. Certainly it would appear to have been an impossible expectation on the church membership, and an intolerable burden on women, to be forced to deal with the issue of women's ordination in such an environment. In this respect it would appear to support Paul Edwards's thesis that what may seem to the church as an inconsistent God is more really an expression of the abiding love of God under changing circumstances.

> 4. Evaluate the position that what may appear as "disjunctive" or contradictory may in fact be the action of a consistently loving God revealing the divine will as flawed human beings mature to the point where new truth can be accepted. Can you think of other instances in which this might be the case?

Joining the World

The Saints have moved a long way, both in theory and practice, from the belief that the elders were "sent forth, not to be taught, but to teach the children of men the things which I have put into your hands by the power of my Spirit" (Doctrine and Covenants 43:4b). Advancing technology brings us not only into our neighbors' backyards, so to speak, but into our neighbors' pews as well. Latter Day Saints have largely moved away from their sectarian, or separatist, stance. Members of liberal orientation have long been accused of being unduly influenced by external religious voices in seminaries and in the larger Christian world. However, it is no less true that many conservative members have been touched by the worldwide resurgence of fundamentalism. While these members would insist that true believers should "join none of them," they nevertheless eagerly subscribe to, and repeat as authoritative, the views conveyed through conservative radio, television, and literature more extensively than at any previous point in Reorganization history. This illustrates the phenomenon that has been noted by many observers of the current general religious climate that people often feel they have more in common with like-minded people across denominational lines than within them.

The theological dialogue has been extended beyond our own boundaries in several ways. Not the least significant has been the informal exposure and interchange arising from the daily existence of the Saints in their communities. Church members, including significant numbers of women, have responded to the counsel to be "in the forefront" and have moved into those organizations committed to bringing the ministry of Christ into the lives of others. As they have done this they have discovered, sometimes to their surprise, that their experience in the church equips them uniquely to assume leadership in those organizations. The association and dialogue with other Christians is bringing an increased appreciation of the Reorganization in the larger community.

The dialogue has also been pursued through intentional means: the attendance of church members, male and female, at seminaries for advanced theological education. While this has been routinely criticized by some, the experience of those who have had such opportunities has universally been positive, and has engendered a heightened respect for RLDS members and the church they represent. Similarly, the invitation of individuals from outside the Reorganized Church to participate as consultants and teachers in gatherings of church leaders has produced nothing but positive results, requiring not the abandonment of any valued RLDS perspectives, but a keener and more informed appraisal of the faith.

It is not too presumptuous to insist that the dialogue must continue, both for the sake of the church itself and for the value of the Reorganization's contribution to such interplay. To yield to a kind of religious myopia, to persist in such denominational and cultural provincialism, either willingly or unknowingly, as we have historically exhibited, would be disastrous. To leap forward a few years in our imagination and consider the implications for a church whose traditional white, European membership finds itself in a minority should provide some hint of the challenge. To consider what it will mean for the church to carry its message to the poor and the dispossessed, those with whom we have essentially lost power to communicate, must press us to prepare for serious adjustments. Carter Heyward underscores the need in the strongest terms:

> Theological narcissism, the preoccupation with oneself and with one's god in one's image—or in the image of one's racial, gender, cultural, or religious roots—is a foundational component of the theological structure of ruling class [read white, affluent, Christian male] privilege.... We should be clear that this tendency, to create divinity in our own image, reflects all of us to some degree. It is not wrong to create theological and christological images of ourselves.... But to leave the matter there is more than abstractly wrong. It is destructive of the created/creative world we share. It is wrong to close the canons at the end of one's own story or that of one's people.[9]

It is discomforting to admit that the focus of Jesus' ministry was with the poor and marginalized. It was not long before the initiative for carrying the early church forward lay in the hands of the affluent and powerful, especially as it was "Romanized" and granted the support of the state. It has remained so to this day. Even theology has been reserved for the articulate and the actively self-expressive, and to those with the most current means of communication, in former days the typewriter but now the computer and the Internet. The poor remain not only disenfranchised but voiceless. The Reorganization, essentially by virtue of practicing its own precepts of stewardship and industry, has largely moved away from its roots. Like the university graduate who finds it difficult to communicate with his or her uneducated parents who sacrificed to send their child to college, we have largely lost the ability to communicate with those who constitute the majority of the earth's population, and whose proportional numbers are increasing. We may need to confess that no theology should be accorded status that excludes the presence and the needs of those who cannot speak for themselves. I am grateful to Robert Mesle for bringing this issue to my attention by quoting John Fry:

> I propose that theologians write theology from the standpoint of the mother in Bombay (or Pittsburgh) whose child has just starved to death. She would not be theology's primary reader, and her situation would not provide theology's subject matter. (But) her rage and grief would provide its angle of vision.[10]

The Tension between Known and Unknown[11]
The imperative to maintain tradition and openness to the future in a creative tension is no longer merely an opportunity but a necessity. We will not be so much concerned with proving our history as we are with bringing meaning to it with a bold and creative act of imagination. This is true, I believe, because the best evidence of the Restoration is not the recovery of the events that are seen as the origins for the movement,

but the actual community that becomes the channel of grace and hope for the men and women whom it touches.

The revelation of God is always perceived and responded to through concrete "particulars." The incarnation of God in Christ is a concrete embodiment rather than a generalized theoretical principle: the nature of human beings in history requires this. As heirs of the Reorganization we perceive great significance in certain of these particulars, and my intention is neither to ignore them, deny them, nor feel pressure to accept them uncritically, as though the response to the divine disclosure of one period in time must be normative for all future history.

Our danger is, that in respecting and living in this particular tradition, we absolutize it, which is a form of idolatry. We are constantly beset by the temptation to claim purity and completeness or eternalness for scripture, doctrine, sacrament, or structure, and impute contingency and imperfection to others.

Every tradition, approaching the ultimate as it does through the concrete elements of history and culture, both illuminates and distorts. There is a sense in which the history of a denomination is the account of its attempt to deal with its distortions, or with its apostasies: of the Roman Catholic Church to deal with its Romanness, of Methodism to come to terms with Wesley, of Latter Day Saintism to place Joseph Smith in perspective. Whoever has striven for or taken pride in "a perfect system to obtain" also has had to beware the temptation to invest finality in that system.

Members of the church respond increasingly to opportunities for research and reflection in the various fields of theology—in the area of church history, liturgics, social ethics, and so on we may find reason for both pride and modesty regarding the tradition in which we participate. We may find ourselves standing under the broad Christian witness in ways that we may or may not have acknowledged, but at the same time making our own particular response to the call of God as we perceive it. The tradition has no validity in its own right. It is a storehouse of memory, a vehicle for understanding, and a resource for hoping. Any vitality it has is in the God whose remembered acts it conveys and whose promises for peace and justice it carries.

W. Paul Jones, from the perspective of a thirty-year association with the Reorganization as a respectful and challenging observer, has expressed the belief that the church stands at the threshold of a rare opportunity to move into the future through a bold yet honest appraisal of its tradition, so that significant themes speak to us in ways that move us fruitfully into the contemporary world:

> A gentle liberalism has provided the World Church leadership with the necessary catharsis to transcend a narrow parochialism. This is no longer an issue. The issue is the degree to which this leadership has been so scarred by the fundamentalist skirmishes that they cannot resee their tradition with creative eyes—reloving its uniqueness into a new vision.[12]

---

5. What opportunities exist for (a) your congregation and (b) you personally to participate with other Christians in dialogue, formal or otherwise? Have these occasions been beneficial for you and for those with whom the dialogue has been carried on?

6. With what aspects of the Reorganized tradition do you feel most comfortable and confident in sharing with your neighbors or friends? What aspects do you feel least comfortable in sharing? Why do you feel as you do? How do you feel if a friend or acquaintance shares some belief with you that you had thought to be distinctive to the Reorganization? Do you feel that this diminishes the authority or uniqueness of the church?

And Still Hazardous

The hazards do not diminish merely by recognizing them. The influences of tradition and usage, institutional loyalty, cultural limitation, and identity anxiety are formidable. In addition, the "natural spiritual inertia" to which F. Henry Edwards referred weighs like a millstone around our necks, or, more accurately, *on* our minds. In critiquing certain Mormon historians, Paul M. Edwards has leveled a charge that may apply to all of us to some degree in our theological inquiry, that "they seem to believe in order not to be forced to know," or that they are scholars who "have gone into history in search of a text for their sermons rather than for an understanding of the past."[13] As suggested by Edwards, the imperative for responsible historians, a "passion for puzzlement," applies equally to those engaged in the theological task.

> These are people who ask themselves, "What is it that we are trying to understand?" and search and interpret in the realization of this query. But it is not just a question of being puzzled. It is more than that. We are talking about what it means to have the feeling of puzzlement. It includes the willingness to seek from the past and from the present and to do so in the hope that the search, even with some error, is the key to tomorrow.[14]

An experience attributed to Moses and described in the Doctrine and Covenants, contains a statement that could provide a dynamic for the Reorganization as we pursue the theological task in a new millennium. Moses is reported as having been exposed to some new insights. As a result, he is forced to confess: "For this cause, I know that man is nothing, which is a thing I never had supposed."[15] It can surely be expected that the future of the church and the effectiveness with which its mission is discharged will rest to a significant degree on the discovery and embracing of things that we have never before supposed.

7. Can you recall the experience of coming to understand something that you "never had supposed"? What was it that you came to understand? How did you arrive at understanding? What feelings did you experience in the process?
8. Do you believe that you might have a similar experience in the future? Do you have any idea what that new understanding might be?
9. The January 1966 issue of the *Saints' Herald* carried an article titled "Current Theological Issues." Are you familiar with the issues described here, and do you have an opinion about them? Has your congregation had opportunity to discuss them recently?
10. One pastor declared that there would be no discussion of controversial issues because of the tensions this might create. How do you evaluate this position?

Activities for the Reader

A. Briefly note *three* ideas or insights that you have found helpful in this chapter. Then note *three* ideas that you found least helpful, or least clearly explained.
B. Make a brief statement concerning what you might do to improve your own theological activity. Then note how you might contribute to the theological activity of the congregation.

Notes

1. The First Presidency, foreword to *Exploring the Faith* (Independence, Missouri: Herald House, 1970).
2. Howard J. Booth, "The Task of Theology," *Saints' Herald* 136, no. 7 (July 1989): 279.
3. The First Presidency, "The Nature of New Revelation," *Saints' Herald* 131, no. 3 (February 1984): 52.
4. *Exploring the Faith* (1970), preface.

5. Paul M. Edwards, "To Be God Is to Appear Changeable," *Saints' Herald* 131, no. 17 (September 1984): 397.

6. *The True Latter Day Saints' Herald* 23, no. 14 (July 15, 1876): 434.

7. *The True Latter Day Saints' Herald* 19, no. 15 (August 1, 1872): 457.

8. *Saints' Herald* 35, no. 45 (November 10, 1888): 713.

9. Carter Heyward, "Jesus of Nazareth/Christ of Faith: Foundations of a Reactive Theology," in Susan Brooks Thistlethwaite and Mary Potter Engel, eds. *Lift Every Voice: Constructing Christian Theologies from the Underside* (San Francisco: Harper Collins, 1990), 197.

10. John Fry, *The Great Apostolic Blunder Machine* (New York: Harper & Row, 1978), 174–175.

11. The following section is an adaptation of a paper titled "Revelation and the Restoration Principle." The paper was first written thirty years ago, published in 1973, and critiqued (kindly but firmly) by Larry Conrad and Paul Shupe in *Dialogue: A Journal of Mormon Thought* 18 (Summer 1985): 92–103. I believe the substance of the paper still has merit, and see no reason to reinvent the wheel.

12. W. Paul Jones, "Demythologizing and Symbolizing the RLDS Tradition," in Darlene Caswell, ed., *Restoration Studies V* (Independence, Missouri: Herald House, 1993), 110.

13. Paul M. Edwards, "The Irony of Mormon History," *Utah Historical Quarterly* 41, no. 4 (1973): 395–396.

14. Ibid., 401–402.

15. Doctrine and Covenants 22:7b.

Preview Answers

Theology Preview

1. F   Doctrine and Covenants 42:12 states that those who "have not faith to be healed, but believe" are to call for laying on of hands for administration.
2. F   GCR 308, paragraph 7 (1886) states that "plenary inspiration" has never been affirmed by the church.
3. F   The doctrine of justification generally refers to the way God accepts sinful persons as righteous, through the death and resurrection of Christ received in faith.
4. F   Immaculate Conception, generally accepted as dogma by Roman Catholics since 1854, is the belief that the Virgin Mary was preserved free from the effect of original sin from the moment of conception by divine grace.
5. F   What came to be known as the Epitome of Faith was part of a letter written by Joseph Smith in 1842 to John Wentworth, editor and proprietor of the Chicago *Democrat*, setting out some of the beliefs of the church. While respected through the years as a useful resource, it has never received official endorsement.
6. F   Strictly, the church has interpreted "healing" in a broader context than physical cure and has declined to assert that recovery from sickness, disease, or other outcomes of our mortality (including death) is directly proportionate to faith.
7. T   The church approved such a resolution in 1894 (GCR 391). The resolution includes a lengthy prefatory statement by the First Presidency and a statement of

belief in twenty-seven words. Theologically, the preface has been of considerably more value than the actual statement of a position on the resurrection, referred to by the Presidency as a matter of "secondary importance."

8. F   The truth or validity of matters of debate or difference are not decided by Conference vote. At the 1910 General Conference Joseph Smith III stated there is no earthly tribunal that can ultimately decide the truth of any matter. Conference votes commit the church to courses of action approved by majorities.

9. F   Eschatology is that branch of theology dealing with "last things," traditionally the resurrection of the dead, the second coming of Christ, final judgment, and life everlasting.

10. T   The predominant view of the Book of Mormon affirms that the Father and the Son are one, as detailed in Alma 8.

Scripture Preview

1. F   The Synoptic Gospels, so called because viewed together they give an interdependent picture of the life and ministry of Jesus, are Mark (considered to be written first), Matthew, and Luke. The prevailing theory is that both Matthew and Luke borrowed from Mark, and also from some other unidentified source referred to as "Q," as well as providing material unique to themselves.

2. F   The Authorized Edition of the Book of Mormon was published in 1908.

3. F   The original dictated manuscript, of which only a very small part survives, is in the possession of the LDS (Mormon) Church. The RLDS Church has pos-

session of the "P" or emended manuscript, prepared from the original for the printer. That part of the original manuscript given to the Reorganized Church deteriorated from the absence of appropriate care and is no longer available.

4. F The exact wording is "to the convincing of the Jew and Gentile that Jesus is *the Christ, the Eternal God.*" Church members often quote this passage wrongly because it coincides with the view of the Godhead that has traditionally been held.

5. F The Book of Mormon has passed through several editions, and contains many corrections and amendments made by Joseph Smith both before and after its initial publication in 1830. The interested student will want to consult Richard P. Howard's book, *Restoration Scriptures: A Study of Their Textual Development*, which is the standard RLDS work in this field.

6. F There are more than 5,000 added or modified verses in the Inspired Version. These changes are detailed in Paul Wellington's book, *Joseph Smith's "New Translation" of the Bible* (Independence, Missouri: Herald House, 1970), an invaluable resource for the student of scripture.

7. T The Book of Enoch, or rather Books of Enoch, believed to have been written around the second century B.C., and attributed to Enoch, have been available in English translation since 1927.

8. T Those who study the scriptures and attempt to understand the meaning of given passages are engaged in exegesis.

9. F Lower criticism is the term applied to the study of manuscripts to determine the most accurate form of the text. Higher criticism refers to the study of the scriptural writings to determine authorship, date of

writing, intended audience, historical background, etc.

10. T   The church acted in this matter in 1878 (GCR 215).

History Preview

1. F   Section 134 (October 1922) calling six men to the Council of Twelve, was approved by a vote of 656 (for) to 452 (against). When the document was first presented on October 2, the Council of Twelve unanimously declined to accept it and the Seventy also declined to approve. The vote was finally taken on October 12. An account of this episode may be found in *Church History*, 7: 480–494.

2. T   Jesse Gause was called and ordained as a counselor to Joseph Smith on March 8, 1832. His name was included originally in what is now Section 80 of the Doctrine and Covenants. He served only briefly, disappeared while on a mission in August of that same year, and was eventually expelled. When Section 80 was printed in the 1835 Doctrine and Covenants, Jesse's name was replaced by that of Frederick G. Williams. No mention of his name in connection with the First Presidency appears in *Church History* or in the introductory notes to Section 80, though both Paul Edwards and Richard Howard make reference to him in their histories.

3. F   On January 21, 1836 (reported in *Church History* 2:16ff.), Joseph Smith was surprised by an experience that convinced him that all individuals who had died, or would die without a knowledge of the gospel, who "would have received it with all their hearts" would be heirs of celestial glory. This was contrary to the widely accepted view at that time.

4. T   At the 1868 General Conference a resolution was introduced to extend the vote to women. A substitute motion, affirming the right to vote of "private members" (including women) was approved after "rigorous examination" and "some lengthy arguments." The matter is reported in the *Saints' Herald* 14 (1868): 126–127.

5. F   The account published at the beginning of *Church History* was not generally known until 1842, when a short account was published in the *Times and Seasons* (March 1, 1842) followed by the more familiar account in the next two issues of this journal (March 15 and April 1, 1842). Richard Howard writes that the grove event "simply was not generally known to the membership during the first decade of the church's life." (From an article entitled "An Analysis of Six Contemporary Accounts Touching Joseph Smith's First Vision" in *Restoration Studies I.*)

6. F   Early Christian writings, notably those of the Apostolic Fathers, identify bishops (who received their commission from the apostles), elders, and deacons as comprising the officers in the early church.

7. F   The members of the Council of Twelve were selected and ordained in February 1835 by the three witnesses to the Book of Mormon. There is no contemporary account of this development, the first published reference being in the *Millennial Star* (Volume 15), nine years after the death of Joseph Smith. The editors of the *Church History* (1:537ff), while assuming the broad veracity of this later account, find it "strange" that the leading periodical of the church at the time (*Messenger and Advocate*) "should not have mentioned events of such importance."

8. F   The earliest accounts indicate that the term "bishop" was first an alternative title for "elder." By the second century the term was reserved for chief or presiding elders in the congregations.

9. F   Several manuscripts comprised the data available to the Reorganization, showing evidence of an ongoing revision of the text, both of the Old and New Testaments. The committee charged with providing for the publication of the record played a significant role in the final determination of the text.

10. F   Although the concept of Zion, the "new Jerusalem" became part of the vision of the church from its earliest days, the symbol was already deeply embedded in the consciousness of Americans, and had been since the foundation of the colonies. The notion featured prominently in sermons, published broadsheets, and political discourse, although its appeal had begun to diminish with the rise of the individualistic spirit in the new nation.

Case Study
Joseph Smith's New Translation
of the Bible

Introduction

This case study is offered as an appendix for the purpose of providing a specific example in theological exploration. This particular subject is chosen for two reasons:

1. The New Translation (or the Inspired Version as it came to be called), has been highly visible in the life of the Reorganized Church. It has been used often as a yardstick for judging the fidelity of any member using the Bible as a resource in preaching or teaching. Not only had the manuscripts come to the church through the faithfulness of Emma Smith, but their possession exerted a strong positive influence on the morale of the scattered Saints coming together from the dispersion following the Nauvoo exodus.

2. Despite the importance ascribed to it, the Inspired Version has received remarkably little careful examination to determine the nature of the "translation." The manuscripts were in the hands of the Reorganization for almost a century before the first known scholarly perusal of the data, and before careful measures were taken to preserve this valuable resource. Church historian Charles Davies, in the study mentioned below, commented on the unexpected complexity of reconciling the several manuscripts, and the committee's difficulty in producing an accurate work when the textual evidence often seemed at odds with the underlying assumption of a text produced by revelation. "It may have been the realization of this complex prob-

lem," he wrote, "which motivated the keeping of the manuscripts in comparative seclusion."

There are at least three values attached to the choice of the Inspired Version for study:

- The process will demonstrate something of the hazardous nature of theological exploration, because the subject deals with sensitive issues for members of the RLDS Church. In his preface to the manuscript analysis Davies wrote: "I have been deeply concerned by the need to present some basic facts in light of a tendency among our people to react strongly to statements which do not tend to confirm deeply ingrained concepts and traditions." Study of the Inspired Version may not be a "safe" subject, but hopefully it can be a fruitful one.
- Although it is not possible to reproduce all the data relevant to the study, some basic references will be cited. Interested members will have some worthwhile avenues to follow.
- The study will suggest some general principles for the Reorganization's understanding of and approach to its scriptural resources. These principles have been addressed in the body of the book but will have particular applications in this case study.

As indicated above, and in several of the available resources, the work done by Joseph Smith has been identified by several names. Joseph himself referred to the "New Translation," although the production was obviously not a work of translation in the normal sense of the word. The name by which the work was identified from the time of its first printing in 1867, including the reference in GCR 215 (1878), was simply the Holy Scriptures. In 1890, when Joseph Smith III was giving evidence in the Temple Lot Suit, he identified it as the "New Translation." In 1936, by a Herald House editorial decision, the name Inspired Version was adopted, although this name had been favored by some members of the church for some years previously. John Etzenhauser used the term "Inspired Version" in his 1903 text of *Three Bibles Compared*. While recognizing its inadequacies the term "Inspired Version" will be used in this case study, unless "New Translation" or "Holy Scriptures" seem appropriate to the context.

A Chronological Listing of Some References to the New Translation

It will be helpful to provide some guides to assist in this study, identifying those who have made statements regarding the Inspired Version. As suggested above, very little is available from the first century of the Reorganization. Most of the material during this time consists of citations from the text, along with the Book of Mormon and Doctrine and Covenants references offering a rationale for another version of the Bible. Interest was stimulated by the approaching centenary of the first edition's appearance in 1867. The following references are pertinent to the study:

1. In 1903 a pamphlet titled *Three Bibles Compared: Scholarship and Inspiration Compared* (Independence, Missouri: Ensign Publishing House) was produced by John Etzenhauser. This resource went through several editions, the most recent acknowledging the joint authorship of Etzenhauser and J. B. Phillips, revised by Paul Wellington (1957). The pamphlet in its most recent edition provided a comparison of selected passages from the Authorized Version, Revised Standard Version, and Inspired Version, designed to illustrate the value of the latter in giving a superior rendering of the text.

2. Garland E. Tickemyer, *The Old Testament Speaks to Our Day* (Independence, Missouri: Herald House, 1960–1961). This approach to a senior high study course reflected views of the historical development of the Old Testament that aroused dissatisfaction among many members, who complained about Tickemyer's apparent neglect of the Inspired Version as the literal restoration of the original text, communicated by direct

revelation.. It was on this basis that the Inspired Version was considered superior to all other versions which allegedly had been corrupted.

3. Richard Lancaster, James Lancaster, and Donald Landon together authored a teacher's manual for Tickemyer's book. The quarter for October–December 1960 included the following statement, implying a different understanding of the text and suggesting that the term "restored" applied to the text be used advisedly:

> There are three types of changes or additions in the Inspired Version arising from three types of "errors" that occur there. The *first* is a correction or amplification that Joseph Smith has added to the thought or theology of the ancient writer.... This is not to imply necessarily that at one time the ancient writer used the words or even had the thoughts that Joseph Smith placed in the text.... We cannot expect, then, to find in the Inspired Version that all of the corrections appearing there were at one time on the lips of the early Hebrew or Christian writers. (pp. 27–28)

4. In the early 1960s, at the request of the First Presidency, church historian Charles Davies undertook a detailed study of the Inspired Version manuscript. His studies, more extensive than any that had been carried out previously, allowed the manuscripts to bear their own witness, as it were, to the nature of the work. Although this study was not published it was highly influential in the understanding of church leaders in the following years. A copy is to be found in the unpublished works holdings of the Temple Library.

Davies titled his study "Problems in the Inspired Version" (1965). The committee of 1867, he wrote, must have been surprised by the complexity of the task they faced in reconciling several documents to produce a final text. One conclusion Davies reached was: "The claim to restore lost parts does not seem to be substantiated at this point on any really helpful basis." (p. 10) The virtual flood of ancient biblical manuscripts coming to light since 1830, Davies suggested, affirmed the high level of accuracy of the text as published in the various editions of the Bible.

5. In the May 1, 1966, issue of the *Saints' Herald*, in the section entitled "Question Time," Richard Howard described in some detail the manuscript data on which the Inspired Version was based. For many readers this was the first time to recognize that the Inspired Version was not a verbatim reproduction of a single manuscript but the product of a complex development in which the committees of both the 1867 and the 1944 printings played significant roles.

6. My own statement, "A Reinterpretation of Inspiration, Revelation and L.D.S. Scriptures," was presented at the church-wide College Student Conference held at Graceland August 26–September 1, 1967, and published in the *University Bulletin* 20 (Winter 1968). This was a preliminary attempt to examine the manuscript and text of the Inspired Version (as also the Book of Mormon and the Doctrine and Covenants) in light of the professed doctrine of revelation being advanced by the church.

In a very short period of time after a century of relative inattention, three resources of great significance in addition to the Davies study were published, all of them readily available to those interested in pursuing the question of the Inspired Version:

7. In the November 15, December 1, and December 15, 1966, issues of the *Saints' Herald*, President F. Henry Edwards wrote a series of significant articles on the Inspired Version. These brought to the attention of readers, for the first time, some basic information and insights concerning the New Translation. The full text of these articles make up an important element of any serious study of the Inspired Version. Among the points made by Edwards were the following (page references are to the reprint of these articles in Paul Wellington's book, mentioned below; it is also available in booklet form as *What Is the Inspired Version?*):

a. The belief that the original text of the Bible had been corrupted was not unique to Latter Day Saints; the idea of a "New Translation" was not unfamiliar (p. 7).
b. The probability that, although the revisions were sufficiently completed for publication, "other evidences indicate the high probability that the manuscript was not 'complete' in the sense that all errors were now eliminated" (p. 10).
c. "Important though the Inspired Version was, it was not vital to the faith of the Saints of the early Restoration.... [T]he King James Version was nevertheless treasured and used. When the ministers were instructed to 'teach the principles of my gospel...' the Bible which they used without hesitation was the King James Version" (p. 12). This was an important point to establish, because there had been a widespread disparagement of other versions, along with the insistence that the Inspired Version should be used exclusively in the church.
d. "Many of the changes were purely incidental (such as 'saith' to 'said'), and other changes were made for smoother reading rather than for any basic difference in meaning" (p. 16).
e. "...it has been thought by some students that the changes made in producing the Inspired Version of the Holy Scriptures were divinely imparted to Joseph Smith in such a manner that he was a willing medium but nothing more. The content of the changes made was held to be of God, with Joseph having no part in them except to transmit them. This does not appear to be borne out by study of the manuscripts" (p. 18).
f. "...there were places where Joseph clearly revised his own earlier revisions. Knowledge of this fact should not disturb us. Rather, it should help us to understand more clearly the part which the prophet plays in the total revelatory experience. When we refer to the Inspired Version of the Holy Scriptures we are referring to the inspiration which enlight-

ened and guided Joseph in his work rather than to some special and final rightness in the words which he wrote" (pp. 20–21).

g. "...study of the Inspired Version of the Holy Scriptures indicates that the spirit of revelation functions at different levels.... This is not written in an attempt to disparage any or all of the Inspired Version. My purpose, rather, is to emphasize the fact that it is the message of the Bible and not the exactness of its verbiage, nor even the manner in which it has come to us, which is important" (p. 22).

8. In 1969 the first edition of Richard Howard's book *Restoration Scriptures: A Study of Their Textual Development* was published. This ground-breaking study examined in depth the part played by the several manuscripts and the committees (1867, 1944) in the development of the Holy Scriptures. Comparisons of the text of the KJV and New Translation, as well as study of the various stages through which the text passed before appearing in print, brought to the attention of the Saints for the first time some crucial insights for evaluating the nature of the work, A second edition, completely revised and enlarged, was published by Herald House in 1995.

9. In 1970 Paul Wellington's *Joseph Smith's "New Translation" of the Bible* appeared. This was a comprehensive, parallel column rendering of the KJV and the IV, allowing comparison of the text. As mentioned above, the three articles by F. Henry Edwards are included as an introduction, followed by 500 pages of parallel columns, giving some idea of the many hundreds of texts changed or added. This is an indispensable resource for anyone intending to become acquainted with the nature of the Inspired Version.

10. Robert J. Matthews, *"A Plainer Translation": Joseph Smith's Translation of the Bible* (Provo, Utah: Brigham Young University Press, 1975, 1985) brought a LDS scholar's perspective to the New Translation. This is a detailed analysis of the text, the manuscript data, and some interpretative commen-

tary. In response to the question, "Is the New Translation a restoration of the original text of the Bible?" Matthews includes a section entitled: "The New Translation may be many things?" (p. 253ff). This coincides with the suggestion of Lancaster, Lancaster, and Landon that one kind of change consisted of additions to the text and/or thought of the original writers.

Some Questions to Consider

Although anyone undertaking a study of the Inspired Version will need to determine his or her own agenda, some questions would appear to belong necessarily to such a study:

a. What do the manuscripts indicate about the process of inspiration and Joseph Smith's use of the term "translation"?

b. Given the nature of the textual changes, the fact that Joseph made many revisions to changes he had made earlier, and the fact that a majority of changes were stylistic and grammatical rather than changes in meaning, how are we to understand the meaning of the 1867 committee's assertion that the work was done by "direct revelation."

c. How would the claim to direct revelation relate to statements by the RLDS Church and by Joseph Smith III that the church did not affirm "plenary inspiration"? Joseph took this position specifically in testifying regarding the New Translation in the Temple Lot Suit.

d. In his 1966 series of articles in the *Saints' Herald*, F. Henry Edwards placed the word "restored" in quotes (p. 22), signifying that the term should be used cautiously. This was the position also adopted by Lancaster, Lancaster, and Landon. If it is correct to accept the point of view that additions in the text may not be actual "restorations" of some original text, but in fact new material, then can *any specific addition* be regarded with certainty as a restoration, or must that decision in every case remain a matter of personal opinion.

e. How many different kinds of changes—stylistic, grammatical, word modernization, conceptual, etc.—are to be found in the Inspired Version? What is the significance, if any, of the fact that some of these ("saith" to "said", "which to "who") are no longer inserted after the end of John 5?

f. Given a growing confidence in the accuracy of the biblical text as transmitted and translated, what attitude should be adopted toward the traditional view of the Reorganization that the King James (Authorized) Version, and therefore all other versions, are corrupted, either by accident or design?

g. The term "Inspired Version," implying the corruption of all other versions, may be burdening the Reorganization with a position that is neither accurate nor charitable. The Reorganization has lived longer with the term "Holy Scriptures" than with either of the terms "New Translation" or "Inspired Version." Would it be possible or desirable to adopt a new title, or to revert to the one originally chosen by the church?

Establishing an Opinion

This specific study, like others, may well be an ongoing process. There may have been resources you were not able to review. However, it may be helpful at the conclusion of such reading and dialogue as you have been able to manage to review your current judgment with respect to the nature of the Inspired Version. One way of doing this may be to compare your opinion against some categories used in a survey some years ago inquiring about belief in the meaning of revelation and the nature of the Inspired Version, the Book of Mormon, and the Doctrine and Covenants.

In that study 274 randomly selected church members were asked to give opinions on the four items mentioned above. In the case of the Inspired Version, subjects were asked to choose from four categories the one which matched their opinion most closely. These categories are listed below, with the percentage of members choosing each category. Determine the category that most closely approximates your current opinion. Results are provided for males and females separately, and for the composite survey group.

Response Alternatives	Males	Females	Total
	(shown as percentages)		
A. The Inspired Version is a revision of the Bible completed by Joseph Smith Jr. under the direction of the Holy Spirit. The additions and changes which were made were given to him through revelation, and the Inspired Version accurately expresses the content of the ancient biblical writings.	47.2	44.9	44.9
B. The Inspired Version is a revision of the King James Version of the Bible, with numerous changes. These changes were directed by revelation of God, and the resulting Inspired Version expresses God's truth more accurately and clearly than does any other edition of the Bible.	41.5	47.8	44.2
C. The Inspired Version contains the apparently unfin-	10.1	7.8	9.1

Response Alternatives	**Males**	**Females**	**Total**
	(shown as percentages)		

ished work of Joseph Smith as he made alterations in the Bible text, under the influence of revelation or inspiration of God, to express his theological and biblical understandings.

D. The Inspired Version is the product of Joseph Smith's subjective appraisal of the Bible. Since most of the revisions were stylistic rather than theological, and since only 5 percent of the King James Version was revised in any way, there is little element of inspiration or revelation in the changes which he made.

	1.3	2.6	1.8

If none of these expresses your opinion to your satisfaction, make a brief statement that describes it more closely. If possible, consider what steps may need to be taken next to improve the basis of your knowledge as a basis for your opinion.